Design of Rail Stations

Steven Boldeman

© Dolans Publishing

Copyright Notice
All rights reserved. This work is copyright. No part of this work may be reproduced, stored in a retrieval system, or transmitted in any form or by any means with the prior written permission of the publisher. Except as permitted under the Copyright Act 1968, for example, any fair dealing for the purposes of private study, research, criticism, or review, subject to certain limitations. These limitations include restricting the copying to a maximum of one chapter or 10% of this book, whichever is greater.

National Library of Australia Cataloguing-in-Publication Data
Creator: Boldeman, Steven Author
Title: Design of Rail Stations
ISBN: 978-0-6483093-4-5

Subjects – Railroads – Planning
Transportation – Planning
Transportation - Australia

Dolans Publishing

For Andrew

Table of Contents

Chapter 1 Introduction 1
Chapter 2 Describing a Rail System 2
    Number of passengers per day 2
    Route Length 2
    Number of Stations 5
    Traffic Type 5
    Power Supply 6
    Gauge 7
    Number of Lines 8
Chapter 3 Types of Passenger Rail Systems 11
    Light Rail Systems 14
    (Classic) Light rail 24
    Heavy Rail 30
    Other Rail Systems 49
Chapter 4 A Very Basic Introduction to Rail Infrastructure 60
    Track 60
    Tunnels 69
Chapter 5 Basic Station Types 77
    Styles and Configurations of Stations 77
    Terminal Stations 84
    Major Components of a Station 85
    Access in and out of Stations 89
Chapter 6 Customer Support on Stations 93
    Passenger information systems 94
    Timetable Information 99
    Tickets and Ticketing 100
    Vending Machines and Advertising 105
    Souvenir Shops 108
    Other Infrastructure 109
Chapter 7 Geometry, Heights and Grades and Platform Gaps 112
    Loading and Structure Gauge 113
    Centre and End Throw 120
    Superelevation (Cant) 128
    Calculating Platform Gaps 129
    Platform Heights 131
    Grades 134
Chapter 8 Nearby Centres and Facilities 138

Shopping Centres *141*
Airports *142*
Carparks *144*
Stadia/Stadiums *146*
Transit Centres *146*
Universities *148*
Theme Parks/Amusement Park *149*
Exhibitions Centres/Conference Centres *150*
Racecourses and other sporting event places *152*
Major Tourist Attractions *153*

Chapter 9 Underground Stations 155

Fire Protection and Safety for Underground Stations *158*
Infrastructure in an Underground Station *162*

Chapter 10 Managing and Modelling Passenger Flows 170

Introduction *170*
Passenger Flow Modelling *172*
Designing for Better Dwells at Stations *182*

Chapter 11 Network Design around Stations 190

Introduction *190*
Detailed Drawing of Rail Systems *192*
Station Network Configurations *196*

Chapter 12 Other Aspects of Station Design 201

Introduction *201*
Exits and Entrances *201*
Concourses *204*
Interchange Stations *209*
Short Platforms *213*
Cover for Passengers from the Elements *215*
Straight and Curved Platforms *216*
Reusing Disused Stations *219*
Light Rail Station Design *221*
*Managing Power Consumption and Station Environmental
Management* *224*

Chapter 1 Introduction

Rail stations are a critical part of any passenger rail system. They are the point where a rail system allows passengers to both board and alight, and there are no other places where this is permitted.

Rail stations are the focal point for many of the services provide for a rail system. It is what passengers see and experience when using a rail system. The overall performance of a rail system is often judged against the quality and type of the stations in use in that rail system. It is very hard to overstate the importance of stations to a rail system.

The area around stations can be developed, and many different facilities can be built around a station. Examples include shopping centres, and commercial buildings. Alternatively, rail systems can be connected to important facilities such as exhibition and convention centres, and these centres can be considered part of the overall station precinct.

Stations impact upon the throughput of trains through a rail system. In many rail systems, such as a metro system, throughput is a very important aspect, and there is a premium on getting more trains through. A well designed station allows for faster and passenger movement, and passengers board and alight quicker. Better station design allows for more trains through a rail system, and this allows for more trains. This aspect of station design means that good station design is a critical part of any rail system with a large number of passengers per day.

Passenger flow through a station is determined by its geometry, and the number of passengers. A more crowded space means that people move more slowly. A high level of crowding can result in very slow movement though a station. Alternatively, where passenger flows cross one another then movement speeds can be substantially affected.

Different rail systems require different things from a station. Some stations require only the mo   st basic services, and more than this is not needed. Other stations have a very high level of service as the number of passengers is very large, or the journey requires much more by way of services.

Chapter 2 Describing a Rail System

There are several commonly used parameters that can be used to almost completely describe a rail system and many of these are described below. Some of them are related to the size of the network, the number of people that use the system, how the system is used by its passengers, and some other useful information.

Number of passengers per day

The total number of passengers is a very important measure. This total is usually calculated from ticket sales, or possibly from the number of people passing through the barriers each day. Normally a work day is used, and weekends are not. Frequently in most rail systems more people use it on a weekday than on a public holiday or on a Sunday.

A person who commutes to work, and then returns home, their trip is counted as two separate trips. A trip is where the person enters the rail system, travels through the system to their destination, and then leaves the system. Where a passenger changes trains, this does not count as two separate trips under normal circumstances. However there are some rail systems when changing trains does count, for example, where two different companies operate trains in the same city, such as Tokyo, or where the passenger changes from one rail system type to another, such as from a metro into a tram.

An alternative name for trips is boardings.

Below is a general guide as to the size of a rail system, and whether it is large or small.

Sizes of rail systems – Number of Passengers		
Trips per day	**Description**	**Comments**
<10,000	Very small	Tourist trains, some tram systems, a small light rail system, an APM in an airport
10,000 to 100,000	Small	High speed rail, most commuter rail systems,

| Sizes of rail systems – Number of Passengers |||
Trips per day	Description	Comments
		small to medium light rail systems
100,000 to 1,000,000	Medium sized	Metros with 2 or 3 lines, large light rail systems, large commuter systems
> 1,000,000	Large	Very large commuter systems, some metros in big cities. No light rail or high speed rail systems move this number of people, nor monorails

Rail as a transport system is capable of moving very large numbers of people. Buses may only move small numbers in comparison, as a reasonable sized bus may move 60 to 100 people, and a commuter train may move a thousand. One of the great advantages or rail systems is the ability to move large numbers of people. A BRT (Bus Rapid Transit) system that has 20 buses per hour, will only move between 1200 to 2000 people per hour for one line in any one direction, and for rail transport this would be considered a very low number. Even the largest BRT systems are small in comparison to a large rail system.

Route Length

The route length of a rail system is an important metric. Rail systems can be very small, but can also be very effective. A small system can move very large numbers of people, especially if it is a metro, even it is quite small. Tram and light rail systems often have a very small number of kilometres of route length, whereas a regional rail system can be extremely large.

Route length is normally measured in kilometres, unless it's in North America or the UK. Care needs to be taken in not confusing route length with track length. The route is the rail corridor where the tracks pass through, and there can be more than one track in any rail corridor. Some rail corridors have many tracks, and up to six is quite common, and some places there are more. There are also some places where trains are stored, and this is called stabling. When counting track length, stabling and marshalling yards can add a lot of kilometres, but for route length add very little.

The table below shows how many route kilometres constitute a large or small system. Again, these numbers are just a guide, and are included to give the reader some sense of what a large or small system looks like.

Route kilometres		
Length	**Size**	**Comments**
< 10 kms	Tiny	One metro line, tourist railway, monorail, airport system
10 – 30 kms	Very small	One or two metro lines, mostly removed legacy tram systems
30 – 100 kms	Small	Many metro systems, many light rail systems, small commuter rail systems, no high speed rail
100 – 500 kms	Medium	Very large tram or light rail systems, commuter rail systems, smaller high speed rail systems
500 – 5000 kms	Large	Large commuter or high speed rail systems, no metros, light rail, monorails nor trams in this category
> 5000 kms	Extremely large	National rail systems, extensive regional train system

Again, what is large for one system can be small for another. High speed rail systems tend to be large, hundreds of kilometres at least, whereas metros are far smaller.

Number of Stations

The number of stations is a key measure for any rail system. The number can vary enormously, as high speed rail systems may have only a tiny number of stations, for example the high speed rail system in Taiwan only has 8 stations. On the other hand, even small tram or light rail systems can have very large numbers of stations, as every street corner can serve as a station. Tram stops are often only 500 metres apart, and a stop on one side in one direction does not mean that there is a matching tram stop on the other side/direction. A tram system of 10 kilometres may have 20 stations.

Even for heavy rail, it is not always clear what constitutes a station for counting purposes. Some stations are only opened at certain times of the year, or for special events. Some stations, especially ones for horse racing or stadia, are only opened when an event is on. There are also small stations where trains do not ordinarily stop, and sometimes these are called halts. A halt is a stop where passengers need to ask rail staff for the train to stop, otherwise the train does not stop. Passengers who need to board a train from a halt need to signal to the driver to stop, and with some luck, this will happen.

Despite the problems with counting the number of stations in a rail system, most of the time it is a very good measure of the size of a system. In most situations a station can be clearly identified from the surrounding track.

Traffic Type

Many, or maybe most, rail systems move only one type of rail traffic. For example, a tram system moves only trams, and does not move commuter or high speed rail traffic. There are always exceptions to this, and some tram systems used to move freight, and there are still a very small number that still do. The different categories of rail traffic types are:

- Light rail
- Trams

- Freight
- Metros (heavy rail)
- Commuter (heavy rail)
- High speed rail
- Others

It should be noted that a rail system that has both passenger and freight traffic is often described as a "mixed" system.

Power Supply

The source of power for any rail system is a very important parameter for any railway. The choice of power source has a large influence on the type of infrastructure that needs to be built to support rail operations. As a rough guide, electricity is provided for rail services where there are large numbers of train movements per day, or for high speed rail. Freight, regional and commuter systems often use diesel power.

Many rail systems are powered through electricity. Steam power was once extremely common as a source of power, but has fallen out of favour with its high maintenance and running costs. The trend away from steam and to diesel and electric power took decades, and by the mid 70s most of the steam locomotives had been removed, although in some parts of the world continued to be used for another 10 years or so. Steam locomotives now are only used on tourist lines.

There are other methods of propulsion other than steam, electricity and diesel power. An extremely small number of rail systems still use cables, where the rail vehicle grabs onto the cable and is pulled along. This type of system was once common, and cables run underneath city streets, pulled from a central point called a powerhouse. One of the last remaining cable car systems is in San Francisco, and this system is still manual, so a tram employee (called the gripman) needs to apply a clamp to the cable to get the street car to move.

Almost all rail systems of interest to the rail planner are either diesel or electric. Diesel systems use diesel fuel to move trains, and electric systems use power generated far away at a power generator to move. Electric systems can be divided into a number of smaller categories, and these are based on the type of electrical power provided. Each rail system can be identified as using one or more power systems that are typically used in a rail system. Power systems are either AC (alternating current) or DC (direct current). AC is now the standard for new rail systems, although the voltages need to be higher, and in some cases this can present a safety risk, so for light rail and trams DC is still preferred. DC is the older power system that previously was commonly used, but now is being slowly replaced with more cost efficient AC power.

Also with the power system almost always a voltage is specified. Common voltages are:
- 750 volts
- 1500 volts
- 3000 volts
- 25,000 volts

The first three voltages are used for DC, and the last one for AC. There are other more unusual ones, but these are the more commonly used voltages. Specifying the power supply for an electric railway requires stating the voltage, followed by whether the power is AC or DC. So specifying a power system would be something like; 1500 Volts DC, or 25,000 Volts AC. The type of power system in use will further influence the choice of trains that are used on the system, and also may increase or decrease the costs and structure of any tunnels constructed.

Where a system has no electricity supply for traction, and there are many of these, then often the system is described as unwired. Power is needed for stations and lighting, but this may be unconnected to traction power.

Many rail systems deliver power through wires suspended over the train, and power is delivered through to the train through a structure on top of the train called a pantograph. However, another structure is also possible called a "third rail", and for this system power is delivered near the ground. This information is also included in any description of a rail system.

Gauge

The gauge of a railway is the distance between the insides of each rail. Most railways have only one gauge, although there are exceptions, such the Tokyo metro. The most common gauge, the one used in the US and for almost all high speed rail, is standard gauge, which is 1435 mm. This corresponds to 4 foot 8.5 inches. Gauges wider than this are normally described as broad gauge, and narrower than this are described as narrow gauge. Common sizes are 1067 mm (cape gauge), and 152 mm (Russian gauge).

Gauge Distance

The gauge distance is measured from the inside of each rail to the other. This measure can change a little when the rail is worn, but for reference purposes the gauge is set for one railway (or line as the case may be).

Almost all high speed rail systems use standard gauge. Most modern installations, except where interoperability with older systems is needed, use standard gauge. Standard gauge is the most commonly used gauge, and more than 50 % of the world's railways, in terms of track length, use standard gauge. The use of non-standard gauges will impact upon rollingstock purchases and decisions.

Number of Lines

The number of lines is a useful measure for any railway. A line is a continuous length of track along which passengers can travel without getting off a train or breaking their journey. In a metro system or a light rail system it mostly very clear how many lines exist, and where lines start and end.

Typically a system with over 6 lines would be considered large, and one with 1 or 2 lines is a small system. Some systems have over a dozen lines.

A commuter system may or may not be described in terms of the number of lines. Commuter lines can converge to a single large station, and there is often shared track where trains from different destinations share the one track. In this situation it can be very difficult to determine how many unique lines there are. In Sydney it is almost impossible to determine how many lines there are as many of the lines meet each other a large distance from the city. Alternatively, in the Go Transit system in Toronto Canada it is very clear how many lines there are because each is mostly separate from each other, and can be easily counted. Again, for a commuter system, more than 6 or 7 lines would be considered a large system.

REFERENCES

1. Zhang, Y & Yan, X & Comtois, C *Some Measures of Increasing Rail Transit Riderships: Case Studies*, Chinese Geographical Science, Volume 10, Number 1, pp 80 – 88, 2000

2. CFL, *Rapport Annuel*, 2011 (In French)

3. Metro de Porto, *Annual Report*, 2009

4. Jernbaneverket, *On Track 2010*

5. State of Florida Department of Transportation, *Central Florida Commuter Rail Transit Design Criteria*, October 2008

6. DB Netze *AG Network Statement 2014*, April 2013

7. Cheng, HY. *High Speed Rail in Taiwan: New experience and issues for future development*, Transport Policy 17 (2010) 51-63, Nov 2009

8. Chun-Hwan, K. *Transportation Revolution: The Korean High-speed Railway*, Japan Railway & Transport Review 40, March 2005

9. Texas Department of Transportation *Austin San Antonio Commuter Rail Study*, 1999

10. Metro de Porto *Annual Report 2011*, http://www.metrodoporto.pt/en/

11. Burge, P. et al Modelling Demand for Long-Distance Travel in Great Britain, www.rand.org, 2011

12. Cataldi, O. & Alexander, R. *Train control for light rail systems on shared tracks*, Railroad Conference 2001

13. Transport for London *Rail and Underground Annual Benchmarking Report* June 2012

14. Prescott, T. *A Practical Scheme for Light Rail Extensions in Inner Sydney*, Transit Australia, vol 63 no 11, 323 – 330 Nov 2008

Chapter 3 Types of Passenger Rail Systems

There are many different types of rail systems, and each has different advantages and disadvantages. When one thinks of rail images come to mind maybe of high speed trains or of metros running underneath major cities. The range of different types of rail systems is actually quite large, and the reader might be surprised as to the variety and large differences between them all.

The distinctions between the different types of rail systems is not always clear. Whilst it is easy to distinguish between a freight system, and a commuter one, things are not always so easy. For example, the distinction between a light rail system and a tram system is particularly difficult, as the different types of systems in many cases are quite different, but in others extremely similar. Some tram systems, especially historical ones, look different to light rail, more modern trams are almost indistinguishable. As such separating out the different types is not an easy task, and an attempt is made here to classify the different rail systems, and it is not possible to consider all the different variations, but nonetheless an attempt must be made.

Rail systems fall under larger headings, and one of those is light rail. This is particularly problematic, as light rail is both a heading and a rail type. This makes things extremely confusing, as the term can refer to either a whole group of different systems, or one particular type of system. The convention that has been adopted to manage this crazy and almost impossible situation is to describe the group of rail systems that fall under the heading of light rail as "light rail systems" and the specific system referred to as light rail as just "light rail".

The choice has been made in this book to separate all the smaller rail systems into the heading of "light rail system". There is no real definition of what this means, especially as a heading, but it is a term commonly used in Australia. It seems clear when looking at the different systems which is a light one, and which heavy, but it is difficult to provide a clear definition. Some of the characteristics of a light rail system include:
- Trains are narrower
- Trains are shorter

- Trains move at slower speeds
- The capacity of any rail lines is lower
- They are physically lighter, and the maximum axle loads can be quite low
- Stations are smaller
- They tend not to have large complex junctions
- They are often much cheaper to construct
- Each individual rail line is quite short, and a maximum line length would be about 30 to 40 kilometres. In contrast high speed rail lines can be hundreds or even thousands of kilometres long.

Alternatively, some light rail systems can be quite expensive to build, especially where the frequency of trains is very high, and the system is driverless. Light rail systems with high capacities can resemble much larger rail systems, and the number of people moved can be reasonably large, ie, one hundred or two hundred thousand per day. The platform heights for light rail systems can also be very low, but in some systems platform height is the same as a heavy rail system.

It is also possible to operate two separate rail systems over the same tracks. Freight trains often share their tracks with regional or commuter trains, and more rarely light rail. Light rail trains can share tracks with heavy rail, so that the infrastructure supports two or potentially more rail systems at the same time. This situation would typically be described as a "mixed system", with at least two different rail systems.

Freight systems fall under neither the light rail system or heavy rail classification, and the particularly serious rail freight systems are called "heavy haul".

To the casual observer the type of rollingstock is often the best way to determine which type of rail system is which. Rollingstock has been designed for each different system, and they look different, so this is quite a good way to start. There are however lots of other system parameters that are also relevant, and the top speed is one, and the number of passengers moved is another.

One of the key distinctions between railways is whether they are "at grade" or "grade separated". Grade separation refers to putting different types of transport modes, or even the same ones, at different heights so that traffic on each can pass one another easily, without having to wait for the traffic to clear an intersection before proceeding. The development of light rail, where trains are often at the same grade as road traffic, has changed the perception that grade separation is always necessary for a rail system.

The photo below shows two grade separated metro lines. This design allows one train to pass over another. For high frequency rail services grade separation is the key to ensuring that trains move smoothly. Where one of the lines crosses another at a junction, the junction may be described as a "flying junction" (as it is in this case in Singapore).

Elevated Metros

Another important distinction between rail systems is the ability of some rail vehicles to have articulation. Articulation is the presence of a joint in a vehicle, so that the vehicle can "bend" around corners and curves. Trucks and buses can be articulated, and rail vehicles also. Light rail vehicles may be articulated, to allow them to turn around very sharp curves. Whilst in the past the lack of articulation in trams was an easy way to separate these vehicles from light rail vehicles, now there are articulated trams as well.

It is sometimes possible to blend two different types of system together. There is no rule that dictates that a rail system must have characteristics from only one type of system, and hybrid systems have been created. Possibly the best known hybrid is the tram-train system that was pioneered in Karlsruhe city in Germany, where trams were re-designed to operate with higher speeds on main line tracks. Nonetheless, having a good understanding of the standard "vanilla" types of rail system can greatly aid the rail planner in developing new transport plans.

Light Rail Systems

Trams

Trams are a very old form of rail transportation. They evolved from the horse drawn carriages that were common in large cities in the mid nineteenth centuries, and were initially steam powered (or pulled by cables). Almost all remaining tram systems in the world are now powered through overhead power lines, where power is supplied from a remote generator to the tram.

Trams are called streetcars in the US and Canada. They are still used in parts of North America, including San Francisco, and Toronto. Trams can be used as simple tourist railways, as they are slow, but a good way of seeing different parts of the centre of a city. Trams may be free in some parts of the centre of large cities, and can be a very pleasing experience to travel on.

Trams were an extremely common system in the Western world until the 1950's, when governments started to remove them. Before their removal they were a central part of the transport for the public for many cities, and some of the tram systems removed were extremely large. The tram system in London was particularly large, and we dismantled with surprising haste in the late 40's and early 50's. Now tram systems are something of a rarity, and very few cities have any kind of remaining tram system. This was particularly the case in the US and Canada, where almost all the old tram systems were removed. Only Toronto and New Orleans operate trams systems that resemble what they were 70 years ago.

In Australia, and the Asia Pacific, the only significant remaining tram system is the one in Melbourne, although there is a much smaller system in Hong Kong that continues to operate for over 100 years. By route kilometres it is the largest remaining tram system in the world, although in the past there were systems that were much larger. The now dismantled system in Sydney was much larger than the one in Melbourne, but has been entirely removed.

Tram systems are rarely double decker (or bi-level) Trams are usually quite narrow, and it is challenging to construct a double decker tram that is both stable and comfortable to use. The trams in Hong Kong are a very rare example of bi-level tram, and offer a quite rough ride.

It is important to distinguish between light rail and tram systems. This distinction is often very difficult to make, but there are significant differences. Light rail is often seen as the logical evolution of tram systems, as light rail is capable of moving more people faster than tram systems. In this book light rail and tram systems are treated as being quite different. Light rail systems often travel in separate rights-of way from road traffic, and sometimes have grade separation as well. Light rail vehicles are also longer than trams, wider, and capable of higher speeds and carrying more passengers. Perhaps the most significant difference between trams and light rail vehicles is that trams are have hard chassis with no articulation, and light rail vehicles are longer and can have many articulated sections. Having said that, many trams are now also articulated.

Trams owe their popularity, and demise, to where they operate. They operate down the centre of streets in the middle of major cities, in what in Australia we would ca
ll the CBD, but in the US would be described as downtown. They are very slow, but are often filled to capacity. This should be contrasted to the situation with light rail, where trains often run on grade separated tracks, or in the middle or roads where road traffic cannot intrude with their separate right of way.

Loading and unloading times on trams can be very long. As there are only a small number of entrances and exists, overcrowded trams can be very slow in moving off from one stop to the next. Trams are not a very effective mass transit system, for moving large numbers of passengers. They are really too small to move millions of people per day, and are really suited for applications where the number of people moved is modest.

Trams also at the same grade as road traffic, and so collisions between trams and cars are possible, and even common. In one year in Melbourne there were over 1000 collisions between trams and road vehicles. Collisions between road vehicles and trams can be very common, and trams need to be strong enough to withstand a collision with a road vehicle from almost any direction. Whilst the collision between any train and road vehicle is serious, it is less serious between trams and road vehicles.

The main differences between light rail and trams are:
- Trams are much shorter than light rail vehicles
- Trams travel down the middle of roads in the centre of cities, something that is often described as being "at-grade", and do not have a separate right of way
- Trams are not connected together
- Trams make a large number of very frequent stops
- Trams are often 2.45 metres wide, whereas light rail is often 2.65 metres wide

Very old trams often look like this one below. This is a heritage tram from Melbourne and is type W class. Note the shape and structure, and that passengers need to step up from the ground to get into the tram. It is also very short, and is only 14 metres in length. It is also rigid, so that there is no articulated section where the tram can bend around corners.

Melbourne W Class tram

Also notice that the tram stop has protection for passengers. Passengers wait of the far side of the fencing, protecting them from road traffic. The gap between the tram and the fence is quite narrow, but this situation is far preferable than having people wait on the side of the road and cross in front of traffic to reach the tram.

The tram shown below is also in Melbourne and was built in the 80's and 90's. It is not single body like the W class, and is articulated to go around corners. This tram still has high floors, but looks more like a conventional light rail vehicle than older trams. In Melbourne this type of tram is known as a B class tram.

Melbourne B Class Tram

This is a tram stopped on Brunswick St in Melbourne. Notice that there is no dedicated tram stop in the middle of the road, and passengers must cross the road from the kerb to reach the tram. Cars are expected to stop before the end of the tram to allow people to board the tram. This situation, very common in a large legacy tram system like Melbourne, is probably mostly unacceptable in any modern tram system.

It was a common feature of trams that passengers had to step up into the tram. This was a major problem for people with disabilities. There has been a major design effort since the 90's to reduce the height of the floor on trams to make them more accessible for wheelchair bound passengers and others who might struggle to climb the stairs. Trams, and light rail, can be classified as ultra low floor, low floor, or high floor. Whilst the low floor design is popular with passengers, maintenance costs are higher. Ultra-low floor trams and light rail vehicles have been plagued with numerous engineering problems, cracked structures and shells, although things do seem to be getting better for this technology.

High Floor Tram

A more modern tram is shown below. This tram is also in service in Melbourne and was manufactured by Alstom in France. Passengers boarding this tram will need to climb from the lowest step to the highest. The tram above is considered to be high floor, as for the purposes of determining if this vehicle is low or high floor, it's high floor because this calculation is made from the ground to the floor of the tram where people are sitting, not to the first step.

Low floor trams and light rail vehicles are typically 300 to 350 mm from the ground to the floor of the tram. Ultra low floor trams that distance can be even lower, even as low as 180 mm. High floor trams the distance is often 550 mm or even more. This distance can be reduced by elevating the surface of the road or sidewalk.

It should be noted that many trams and light rail vehicles which are low floor are not low floor throughout the entire vehicle. Where the bogies are located the floor may be raised, so that passengers moving through the tram will need to walk up and down steps to get from one end to another. This is undesirable from the perspective of passengers with disabilities, but better than having high floor where disabled passengers can't get on at all. Where the tram is only partly low floor, passengers with limited mobility will need to stay near the doors, as they can't move up and down throughout the steps that are in the vehicle.

The percentage of floor area that is low floor is an important percentage for any tram or light rail vehicle. A typical number seems to be about 70%, although the number can be lower than 50% or up to 100%. This figure is important in purchasing any tram or light rail vehicle.

Given the obvious convenience of low floor trams, why was anything built with a higher floor? Surely it made more sense to design all the trams and light rail vehicles with a low floor? The answer to this is that it was only recently that the technology was available to design a low floor tram. High floor rail vehicles structurally stronger, and trains with higher floors are stronger than those with lower floors. So very long trains and definitely those over 100 metres in length, will need to have high floors. Even comparatively short trains, such as the DLR or the Bangkok Skytrain, which are only 60 to 80 metres in length have quite high platforms, as it is easier to design trains with higher floors. Rollingstock manufacturers are designing stronger and stronger vehicles, which can combine low floors with longer trains, but there are still limits on the length of these trains.

Note the significant differences between this tram, and the ones above, it has a much lower floor, is articulated in several places, and looks a bit "space age". This particular tram had very few seats, and most of the space inside was for standing passengers. It was also 100% low floor, and there were no steps other than the one into the tram.

Low Floor Tram

The vehicle in the photo above is a good example of rail vehicles that can be on the boundary between light rail and trams. Given where the vehicle operates, and its width, and the average speed, its probably best to consider this vehicle operating as a tram, even though there are signs and advertisements throughout Melbourne describing this vehicle as light rail.

The photo below shows tram tracks running down Bridge St in Melbourne. Notice that the street is very wide and that trams and road vehicles have a separated right of way. Trams are free of interference from road traffic, and most of the system in Melbourne is like this. This good design is a key reason why the tram system in Melbourne was able to survive, and it's crucially important for any new tram system to be separated from road traffic as much as possible.

Separate Right of Way for Trams

Most trams are only one level, but there are a small number of systems with double decker trams. Trams in Hong Kong are double deckers. This system is a very old system, and operates wooden double decker trams with two sets of stairs at either end of the tram. There is not much suspension, and it's a very bumpy ride. The cost of a ride is very low, somewhere around 40 US cents (as of 2012), and it's extremely heavily used. These trams operate at amazingly frequent intervals, and there are hundreds of trams in use at any one time.

Double Decker Tram in Hong Kong

The tram system in Hong Kong seems a bit neglected, and there were and still are a lot of ways to improve it. One very significant problem was that tram stops were often not located at traffic lights, but often 10 to 30 metres before the intersection. One result of this is that trams stop to let people out, then travel a short distance to the traffic lights, and then stop again. Tram stops should be located at traffic lights, so that when stopped at the lights people can still board the tram, and the tram does not need to accelerate and then stop at the traffic lights.

A modern trend has been to install computer control over traffic lights so that trams get priority. Infrastructure is installed to detect the presence of any tram, and then change the lights to allow the tram to proceed sooner than the normal sequencing of the lights would allow. This situation is particularly common for light rail, where the number of road crossing is much lower than for trams, and the intention is to get the train moving as fast as possible. So doing can substantially increase the average speed of trams, and this is a good way to improve the quality of the system.

An interesting feature of tram systems, and this is especially true for Melbourne, is that often tram stops are marked only with sign, and nothing more. Tram stops are not really stations, and are very low key, and those new to an area with trams may not even notice that the tram stop is there. Stations for other types of rail systems, even light rail, are much larger and more expensive to build.

As a guide for the design of new tram systems, it's best if:
- Trams operate on separate right of ways from road traffic
- Critical intersections are identified and equipment installed to give the tram priority over other road traffic
- Tram stops are located at traffic lights, where there are traffic lights along the tram route
- Passengers are provided with a place to stand next to where the tram will stop
- Trams should be located in central areas of cities or in places where the population density is very high.

(Classic) Light rail

Light rail is seen by many as the next evolutionary step in the development of tram systems. Light rail vehicles are usually larger and longer than trams, and several vehicles can be combined into one longer train, something that is unusual for trams. Whilst there does not seem to be any formal definition anywhere that supports this rule, it seems that light rail vehicles are normally 2.65 metres in width, which is larger than the 2.4 metres common for trams.

Light rail vehicles are designed to travel along city streets. They can climb steep grades, and turn through very tight curves, much like trams. They are a very versatile train type, and can go almost anywhere. Light rail vehicles can climb grades of 10%, and almost unthinkable grade, and far more than any other rail system other than a ratchet and pinion rail line. Light rail vehicles can also negotiate around very tight curves, and curve radii of as low as 20 or 30 metres is possible. Heavy rail is often limited in the size of the curve, and a typical lower value for the tighest curve is 200 metres.

The picture below shows the light rail vehicle moving through central Sydney. Notice that it is a larger and wider vehicle than the trams pictured above. Whilst trams are often only 25 to 40 metres in length, light rail vehicles can be much longer than that, up to 60 metres, and can be coupled together to form even longer trains. This particular light rail vehicle is not designed to be coupled with other light rail vehicles.

Light Rail in Sydney

Once again we note that light rail vehicles can operate on city streets, and building a rail line with a shared right of way with road traffic can be a very effective way to save money in construction costs. As always it is better if the rail line is separated from road traffic as this allows average speeds to be higher, as there is no need for light rail trains to stop for road traffic, although achieving this is sometimes very expensive and not economic.

It is important to distinguish between classic light rail, and an intermediate capacity metro. The DLR (Docklands Light Rail) is often classified as light rail, and it is a light rail system, but it is much more like an intermediate capacity metro, and has many of the features of one. It is not considered to be classic light rail within this book. Specifically, the DLR is fully automated and there are no drivers, and it does not operate down city streets, but is fully grade separated. The DLR is a very good system, re-classifying it as an intermediate capacity metro is no insult. This type of system will be discussed further below, under the correct heading.

Light rail vehicles traditionally have drivers. They are important because light rail vehicles need to avoid street traffic, and collisions. At the time of writing it is not possible to design a light rail system that is able to avoid street traffic and pedestrians in all situations, so drivers are needed. Light rail vehicles are designed to be able to withstand an impact from a road vehicle, and are toughened up to resist collisions and not allow any injury to the passengers inside. This toughening can add a lot of weight to the vehicle.

Light Rail in Hong Kong

Light rail has become very popular in the US, and in Germany, although it exists in many different countries. The pictures above and below show a light rail system in Hong Kong. Note that the system used there has high platforms and vehicles are not joined together (amalgamated together) to make longer trains.

The main attraction of light rail systems is the relatively low construction cost. Costs are lower because the light rail trains travel along city streets, and expensive tunnelling an be avoided. Light rail is also a solution where the number of passengers is not that high, and there is a need or desire to install a rail system. Heavy rail systems are excessive in many situations, and a light rail system is a more appropriate solution. Aside from the lower construction cost, light rail is seen as a sexy and attractive looking system, and this type of rail system has proved very popular with passengers throughout the world.

An added advantage of the light rail system is its simplicity. Unlike heavy rail, which is technically very complicated, light rail is a lot simpler and easier to install and manage. Lower speeds, and the lower loads associated with smaller trains, means that the system is relatively simple to install, and the complexity associated with speed calculations and vertical curves for example is avoided.

Automated People Mover

Automated people movers (APMs) are automatic trains that are driverless, and operate on separate right of way with grade separation. They are often very small and often installed in airports, theme parks, and other large facilities. These vehicles fall within the family of light rail systems, and are common in airports in Asia. Also sometimes included in this category are larger automatic trains such as the Docklands Light Rail (DLR), which is driverless, and technically speaking an automated people mover. Larger APMs are very similar to light metros, or intermediate capacity systems, and are also discussed under that category.

The picture below shows an APM in Singapore. The vehicle is very short, and it runs on rubber tyres. It is also driverless, and moves around the small network by itself picking up and dropping off passengers. This particular system is a contained within an airport. The capacity of this system is not large.

An APM Vehicle in Singapore Airport (Changi)

Airports often have trains that move travellers from one terminal to another. A particular large airport may need such a system, as the distances between terminals are so large that transport is needed. These rail systems can be quite significant, and the system in Hong Kong Airport contains two short lines. The APM in Changi airport has several lines, all of them quite short. APM systems in airports are provided as a convenience for passengers, and add to the value of the airport. APMs also exist in theme parks, particular large ones such as the different Disneyland parks.

Intermediate Capacity Metros

Intermediate capacity metros are a system that is designed much like a metro system, with few seats, low headways, and many doors to allow fast and easy boarding and alighting, but much lower capacity and smaller trains. Some intermediate capacity metros are also Automated People Movers, some are not. As a group these rail lines are sometimes described as a "light metro".

What distinguishes an intermediate capacity system from a full metro is:
- Trains are less than 60-70 metres in length
- The trains narrower than full metros
- Stations are much shorter in length, therefore cheaper to build

- In some cases built with rubber tyres rather than metal wheels, although there are some full sized metros with this technology too

Intermediate capacity metros seem to be increasing in popularity, and their numbers are slowly increasing. There are a few rail systems of this type of system in Asia, and the Bangkok Skytrain is probably the best example. The picture below shows a train in the Bangkok Skytrain.

Bangkok Skytrain

There is much to recommend these systems. They are often extremely cheap to build, and well below the cost of a metro system. The Bangkok Skytrain was constructed at a cost of only $20 million per route kilometre, and amazingly low price, and this cost was achieved in 2009 to 2011, relatively recently. Trains in an intermediate capacity metro are also very short, 50 to 60 metres is common, and so purchasing rollingstock is very cheap. Stations in an intermediate capacity metro are also short, and an 80 metre station would be considered large. As such it is easy to place stations in convenient places, as they are so short. Stations are also cheap to build.

Intermediate capacity metros would normally be classified as light rail systems. Recall with light rail systems, the lower capacity of this type of system means that the total capacity in people per hour is lower than a metro. A medium capacity system will usually have less than half the capacity of a metro, maybe even a third, and so there is a significant risk of severe overcrowding. Intermediate capacity metros often operate full, even late at night and on weekends. This type of system is attractive to use because of its cost and versatility, but is frequently overcrowded, a trade-off that is sometimes worth making.

Intermediate capacity metros are commonly installed on concrete viaducts, which makes them cheaper than tunnelled full size metros or at least in South East Asia that seems to be the case. It seems common to install this type of system in elevated viaducts, and this also reduces the cost compared to tunnelling. Intermediate capacity systems can operate at very low headways, similar to metros, or much longer ones, such as one train every 10 minutes.

Heavy Rail

Heavy rail systems have much longer trains, move more people faster, and longer distances. It would be very surprising for a light rail system to move passengers one hundred kilometres from one large city to another. Heavy rail systems are more expensive to build, and ordinarily require a larger space (structure and loading gauge).

Metros

Metros are the mainstay of many transport systems. There are hundreds of metro systems installed around the world, and they have been installed in places such as Algiers and San Juan in Puerto Rico. Many more systems are currently being built.

The metro has become the standard for transport around large cities. The metro system forms the backbone of any transport system in many large cities, and bus lines and other forms of public transportation integrate into the rail system. The key to the success of the metro is its ability to move large numbers of people quickly and efficiently from one place to another, as well as its engineering simplicity, and relatively low cost of operation.

Metros almost always have very few seats. People need to stand most of the trip, and consequently many people can be packed into a metro. More people can stand than sit, and seating takes up a lot of space. The number of people that can be moved by a large metro is extremely large, over 70 thousand pph (people per hour) in one direction, and this can be done at relatively low cost. The ability of a metro system to move such large numbers of people quickly is one of the key reasons why this system has become so successful. The cost of operating a metro system can also be low when compared to the number of people moved, and in very busy cities it may be possible to operate a passenger service at a profit, without any kind of government subsidy.

Metro trains also have a large number of doors. Metro rail carriages are never double decker (bi-level) and so can have large numbers of doors. Dwell time is an important concept for many rail systems, and it is the time a train spends at any one station waiting for passengers to alight and board. The minimisation of dwell time is critical to getting trains through a rail system quickly, and on many different types of system, especially commuter systems, the dwell time can be very long. Metros have very low dwell times because there are lots of doors and people can move into the train quickly as most people stand. The low dwell time of metros is another constituent to their success.

Inside a Metro

The picture above shows a metro train in Hong Kong. As with many metro trains, there are seats along the side of the train, and none in the middle. This allows a very high concentration of people in the train.

Metro trains mostly move along a single line, starting at one end, finishing at another, and then returning along the same path. More unusually, the metro line may bifurcate, and split into two, with maybe half the trains going to one terminus, and the other half to the other. This is different from a commuter system, or a light rail system, which often has a main station where many of the services converge, and passengers can make their way from one service to another quickly and easily. Metro lines do not converge to a central terminus, and so passengers that need to use more than one line must change trains at a large interchange station. These interchange stations usually have the metro lines passing over and under one another, so that passengers need to use stairs or escalators to move up and down to get to the right platform. This is one of the main disadvantages of metro systems, but can be managed quite effectively with good station design.

Metros often achieve a very high level of reliability. Metro trains are almost always on time, mostly due to the simplicity of the system, and that metros operate grade separated from other road and rail traffic. As metros run backwards and forwards all day, from point A to B and then back again, there is very little track infrastructure needed and so there are very few engineering failures. A metro can be compared extremely favourably with commuter rail systems which are often plagued with problems and are frequently late. An on-time-running (OTR) figure of over 99% is the minimum for a properly maintained and operated metro.

Metro trains are not physically very high. They are mostly low and 3.5 metres in height from the bottom of the wheels to the top of the roof would be considered normal for a metro train. This allows tunnelling costs to be significantly reduced, as the size of the tunnel that needs to be excavated is smaller than for commuter trains, especially double decker commuter trains.

Metros can move immense numbers of people. Most rail systems can only move 10 to 15 thousand people per hour (pph) in one direction, but metros can move 60 to 80 thousand in an hour. Some metro lines in Asia and other countries can move over 1 million passengers per day, a truly enormous figure.

Metro systems can have a powerful effect on transport within a city. A good quality metro can clear the roads and allow cars to move through cities very effectively. Even a small number of metro lines can have this effect, and 3 or 4 metro lines is usually enough for cities with even 5 to 6 million people. Hong Kong, which has 3 metro lines and some other lines that are basically commuter lines, is well served with only 3 (although at the time of writing more are under construction). The same can be said for Taipei, where the city has effectively 3 metro lines and one medium capacity line (although they claim there are many more lines than that, essentially there are three main ones). The utility of metro lines is often very high, and even a small number can transform transport within a city.

It is not appropriate however to use metros for long distance travel. As most passengers stand, a metro that travels for hours would require passengers to stand for hours, and many people can't or won't do this. High speed and regional trains are never metro trains. So the question arises as to how far passengers will be able to stand when travelling on a metro line, and whilst no one seems to have written or researched this topic, perhaps the answer should be about 30 to 40 minutes.

Metro lines seem to be getting longer and longer. Traditionally metro lines where quite short in length, and lengths of 10 to 15 kilometres were common. For example, the longest line in the Paris metro is only 24 kilometres long. The author used to believe that one of the lines in Shenzhen was far too long, at 41 kilometres in length, and then another line was constructed in New Delhi that was 49 kilometres long, and another line is under construction in Malaysia that is 51 kilometres long. There is even a line being extended in Shanghai, which was completed in 2010, which is over 61 kilometres long. It is one recommendation of this book for cities and countries not to do this, as passengers must endure hours of travel standing, and will be reluctant to do so.

The reader should remember at this point that metros typically average 35 kms/hr, which can be higher or lower depending on the spacing of stations. A line that is 60 kilometres in length may require someone to stand for 2 hours to get from one end of the other, and even more if they need to change trains and use another metro line. Older people and those with disabilities will have difficulty in completing this type of journey, as standing for hours may be difficult or even impossible.

The picture below is of a metro station in Taipei. This type of open layout for a metro station is a little unusual. Note the platform screen doors.

A Busy Metro Station in Taiwan

Metro systems may or may not have drivers. Older systems will have drivers, but a more modern approach has been to build systems that are entirely automatic and require no drivers. As metro trains are usually captive along one line, and underground, it is relatively easy to program a computer to drive the train. Often rail staff are on board the train, and may control some aspects of the train operation such as opening and closing doors and making announcements. In this case rail staff are described as "operators" rather than drivers.

The design of stations in a metro system is very important. The large number of people present in the system, and on each train, means that it is very important to get people on and off trains quickly. The key to designing a good metro station is to allow people to move freely in both direction, and this often involves separating passengers walking through the station in different directions. The correct design of stations is very important for metro systems, as most stations are underground, and so there is a rick of fire. Also the large number of people using the system means that dwell times can be very large is the station is not designed with care.

Metros can operate at very short headways, 2 ½ minutes is common. Another common headway between successive trains is 5 minutes. This extremely high frequency of trains contributes much to the popularity and convenience of metro systems.

Commuter/Suburban rail

Commuter rail is a rail system where passengers are moved from an outlying area into the centre of a city, and then back out again. Commuter rail is often considered a rail system for working people, as most trips occur on weekdays. Commuter trips are often from suburban stations far from the centre of the city, to the business centre, and then back out again at the end of the working business day.

Commuter trips are often 1 hour or more in length. Commuter trains have lots of seats, and are not metros, so most people are not expected to stand. It is often the case that people stand on a commuter train, but often this is only for the last few stops before the train reaches the centre of the city.

Commuter trains differ significantly from metros. Commuter trains often travel at higher speeds than metros, a common maximum speed for a metro is 90 kms/hr, whereas commuter trains often reach speeds of 130 kms/hr or even faster. Commuter trains are larger, heavier, and longer and often longer than metro trains. The additional speed requires a heavier and more powerful train. Commuter trains also have extensive seating.

The train below is a commuter train in Brisbane (in Australia). This one is on an elevated concrete viaduct, and at Brisbane airport.

Commuter Train on a Viaduct in Brisbane

Commuter trains can be either single or double deck. Double deck trains are common for commuter trains, especially in Europe, and also the US and Canada. Double deck trains can be an effective way of increasing the capacity of a rail line, as more passengers can be seated for one carriage. Double deck trains are used extensively in the Sydney rail system as well.

The photo below is of a double decker train in Paris.

Parisian Double Decker Train

Commuter trains may operate on a large number of different stopping patterns. The stations that a service stops at is called the stopping pattern, and there are many different possible combinations of stopping patterns even on quite simple lines. A metro system, and light rail, trains almost always stop at every station. With any commuter line there are sometimes stations where very few people board and alight from, and so not every train needs to stop there. Commuter trains, because of the large distances they travel, will need to travel as quickly as possible, and not stopping at smaller stations can reduce the travel time. This is common with commuter systems.

The need for up to date information on a commuter line is very important. Again, as commuter services may not stop at every station, passenger information systems need to display where the train will stop, and when it will arrive at the station. As commuter systems can be very complex, and therefore difficult to understand for passenger, and trains can move in many different directions, providing prompt and accurate passenger information is very important in a commuter system, as it is in any rail system.

The photo below shows the inside of a commuter train in Brisbane. This configuration is 2 x 2, and most of the space inside the train is taken up by seating. This is common for commuter trains.

Inside a Single Deck Commuter Train

Commuter systems often have a large central station where all the commuter rail services converge. Easily the most famous of these is Grand Central Station in New York, which has the largest number of platforms of any station in the world (but not the largest number of passengers). Metro systems do not converge to a single station, and this is often a good way of distinguishing the difference between the two different types of rail system.

Commuter rail systems often have much more rail infrastructure than metros and light rail. At the main station for a commuter rail system there are many tracks that carry trains to the station, and many points to move trains to the right platforms. The infrastructure at a main station can often be very extensive to install and costly to maintain.

In a small number of commuter systems trains can be split between 1st and 2nd class. Different fares are charged for each, and more comfortable seating is provided in 1st class. Hong Kong has such a commuter rail line (it's not really a commuter line, as it goes to the border with mainland China, but close enough) with two classes. Passengers in 2nd class get metro style seating, which is very limited and not comfortable at all, and in 1st there are quite "standard" fabric seating in a 2 x 2 arrangement. The fare for 1st class is double that for 2nd class.

Again, comparing commuter systems to metros, most commuter rail systems operate above ground. In the centre of the city, there are sometimes some stations below ground, but most stations away from the centre of town are above ground. Commuter systems are longer and larger compared to metros, and can be over 500 routes kilometres in length. The commuter system in Sydney is over 800 route kilometres in length.

Commuter systems almost always have drivers. The long distances commuter trains travel makes automation difficult, and drivers are almost always used. There are often other staff on the train as well, a guard who opens and closes doors, or a ticket conductor that goes through the train can collects tickets. Commuter trains are more difficult to drive than metros, along the rail corridor many things can happen that require intervention by a driver. There can be landslips, or animals on the track, or trespassers. Trees may fall over onto the track when winds are high. These problems are more uncommon in light rail systems that are commonly confined to urban areas, and metros that are mostly underground.

Commuter systems often share rail tracks with freight. Commuter trains operate at low frequencies and over long distances, and so it is often not economical to separate commuter lines from freight ones. Commuter lines that have freight trains as well typically cannot have a lower capacity, as freight on a rail line has this effect.

Commuter trains mostly do not have toilets, unlike regional services that can have them. Commuter trips are typically about 1 to 1.5 hours and this is considered short enough that toilets do not need to be provided on the train.

Commuter systems can have a very low service frequency, and one train every 20 or 30 minutes or is quite common. In some places one train every hour is considered acceptable. Timetabling becomes very important in this environment, as passengers need to plan to meet the train they need.

Regional rail

Regional rail services are those that move from a large city or town to remote or rural towns or villages. They can be, but often are not, commuter services, and regional services can have travel time of up to 3 or 4 hours. Regional services can be very infrequent, from one every half an hour to one per day. Regional services always have a driver, and maybe other staff on the train. Some regional services may have toilets, or even a buffet car where light refreshments can be ordered.

In Australia regional services often pass through areas of national park and wilderness, where there are large numbers of animals and very few people. Collisions with animals are frequent. There is often no mobile phone reception for large parts of the trip for regional services.

Sydney Regional Train

The photo above is a regional train. Note the clear differences with the other doubler decker trains displayed in this book, the much smaller doors, and the greater overall length of the carriage. Loading and unloading of passengers can be very slow for a regional train, but that doesn't necessarily matter because regional services move only moderate numbers of passengers, and the trip length is commonly 3 to 4 hours. It is preferable to design small doors because this increases the structural strength of the train. Carriages in a train designed for regional services can be very long because this reduces the overall cost of procuring the train.

Regional services can be powered by either electric power, or the train can be propelled by diesel motors. Many regional services are diesel powered, as there is relatively little rail traffic on many regional lines, and the cost of installing overhead power cannot be justified. Where trains are powered by diesel, then a refuelling depot is needed to top up trains when they run low on fuel.

The photo below was taken at Southern Cross station in Melbourne. This regional train was destined for Albury. Note the locomotive pulling coaches, and the locomotive is clearly diesel powered. In this case the carriages behind the locomotive are sometimes referred to as coaches, as they are unpowered. This configuration is often used for regional services as it is cheaper then electric multiple units (EMUs), or diesel multiple units (DMUs)

Melbourne Diesel Hauled Regional Train

Regional services often operate with very few passengers, and as such don't generate a lot of revenue. Many regional services are provided as a community service, and so are not profitable, and need government subsidies to continue to operate. The regional services that the author has seen in Asia, such as in Thailand, Taiwan China and Malaysia, and in Australia are often dirty and not really very pleasant at all, but provide a basic service to those living in remote places with small numbers of people.

High Speed rail

High speed rail (HSR) is a flashy, sleek and sexy system that is often thought of as being very glamorous. High speed rail is often defined as being any rail system where the train reaches 200 kms/hr, or 125 miles per hour.

High speed rail can be divided into two broad categories; trains/systems where trains travel at less than 250 kms/hr but over 200 kms/hr, and those that travel above that. Below 250 kms/hr, HSR trains are sometimes diesel powered, and do not have the extreme aerodynamic streamlining that gives high speed trains their futuristic look. The more sophisticated high speed rail systems all have top speeds in excess of 250 kms/hr, alternatively HSR rail vehicles that use existing lines have top speeds mostly below 250 kms/hr. Some high speed trains are designed to tilt, although most are not. At high speeds tilting as a strategy is not effective for high speed trains.

Below is a high speed train in Taiwan. The high speed trains in Taiwan are based upon a Japanese design. The train used was based on the 700 series Shinkansen.

Taiwan High Speed Train

High speed rail is often considered to be the "best" or most glamorous type of rail system. Its speed and convenience often contribute to this perception. The installation of high speed rail often refreshes and renews the rail system in a country or region. High speed rail sometimes codeshares with airlines, so that passengers can buy a ticket that combined flights and rail trips.

While most high speed trains are single deck, there are a small number of double deck high speed trains. The Japanese have the E4 Shinkansen, and the French have the TGV duplex, but other than those specific trains, all other high speed trains are single deck. Double deck trains have higher capacity, but the stairs in a double deck train can present problems for passengers with luggage.

High speed trains are almost always powered through overhead power, at 25 kV AC. DC power cannot propel trains at high speeds, as high voltages are needed, and diesel trains can only reach about 250 kms/hr, with difficulty. The higher voltages are needed to drive trains to higher speeds.

High speed trains can be very comfortable. The rail infrastructure that supports the train, such as the track, sleepers and ballast, needs to be very strong and in very good condition so that trains can operate smoothly. This results in a very smooth ride quality that provides very little sensation of movement to passengers. Walking around the train is easy, because the ride is so smooth, and some high speed trains have buffet or dining cars where passengers can get meals.

It is a great achievement for a country to install a high speed rail system. Despite the volume of discussion in Australia and other countries concerning high speed rail, very few systems have been installed. There is only one small high speed line in the US, and it operates at around the 200 kms/hr mark, and so does not have the glamour of the French or Japanese systems. Even in the UK there is only one dedicated high speed rail line, which links the Chunnel to London.

Countries where there is a large high speed rail system are, at the time of writing of this book:
- France
- Germany
- Spain
- China
- Japan
- South Korea

- Taiwan

Other countries have smaller parts of a high speed rail system, one such country is Sweden, where a lot of research has been conducted into high speed rail, despite the small size of their high speed system. The line between Moscow and St Petersburg also has some high speed trains, but the line is shared with freight, and this has a big impact on the movement of high speed trains.

High speed rail systems face many technical challenges. High speed trains are moving too quickly to turn or corner quickly, and so can only move through very high radius curves. This often means that high speed rail systems cannot move around mountains and other obstacles, so the rail line often passes through mountains and over other natural obstructions. The alignment of a high speed rail line is very inflexible, and the line can only be designed around any kind of natural barrier with great difficulty.

Tunnels present all sorts of problems for high speed trains. Tunnel design for high speed trains requires the consideration of air movement caused by the train as it moves through the tunnel. The pressure of the air in front of the train is higher than behind the train, and the faster the train goes the worse this problem gets. The pressure drop can cause discomfort to passengers, as the pressure inside the train will equalise with the pressure alongside the train. Lower air pressures will cause passengers to experience pain in their ears. What is commonly done is to seal the train as much as possible, but even so the seals are not perfect, so the pressure will drop in the train as it passes through the tunnel. Sealing the train can reduce the impact of pressure changes to passengers, but in particularly long tunnels the pressure drop will be significant, even in a well designed train.

High speed trains moving through tunnels can cause an effect often described as similar to sonic boom, and the boom can be heard at the exit of the rail tunnel. A high speed train entering the tunnel will generate a pressure wave, which creates the sonic boom. A number of design features can be installed into tunnels to attempt to mitigate this problem, but the most effective strategy is to reduce the speed or the increase the cross-sectional area of the tunnel through which the train is moving. In many cases neither of the strategies will be available.

High speed trains in Taiwan and Japan have very interesting ticketing systems. One feature of these systems is that passengers can buy either first or second class tickets, and first class is more comfortable than second class. But the major difference with "normal" ticketing is the difference between a reserved seat and a non-reserved seat. Reserved seats are those where a seat number is allocated, and these are more expensive that non-reserved. The risk with a non-reserved ticket is that a seat is not available, and it is possible that a passenger may have to stand for part or all of their trip.

High speed rail systems often have trains that have different stopping patterns. All stops trains alternate with express services, and passengers will want to take the service that takes the minimum time to get to their destination. Prices can be different between HSR trains with different stopping patterns, those trains with more stops are often cheaper.

Given the appeal and popularity of high speed rail, it is surprising that more of these systems have not been installed. High speed rail competes effectively where the total travel time between one major city and another is 3 hours or less. High speed rail is particularly effective where the travel time is 2 hours or less. When this is so, high speed rail can be so dominant that air services between the two cities is discontinued, for example, Paris and Brussels. Where the travel time is less than 3 hours but more than 2 between cities, then air services will continue but will have a small percentage of the overall market.

Where the travel time is over 4 hours, high speed rail is no longer competitive with air travel. The trip time is simply too long. Many (or most, depending on the type of engine) planes travel at approx 850 kms/hr, less for turboprop planes, but at that speed a trip of 1000 kms is slightly over an hour. For a high speed train, whilst the top speed can be 300 kms/hr, and for longer journeys the trip duration can become very long. High speed rail will only have a small percentage of the market for trips of this length.

The attraction of high speed rail for passengers, compared to air travel, is:
- Trains are more spacious than planes
- HSR trains do not bounce up and down due to turbulence
- Trains are far less affected by weather than planes, which can be grounded in bad weather
- There are no baggage limitations to high speed rail

- The rules for security for planes don't apply, for example, taking more than 100 ml of liquid onto a high speed train is fine
- There is much less security needed for trains than for planes as the security risk is lower, so security procedures are easier
- Some people have phobias regarding air travel, and prefer to take trains rather than fly
- It is possible for business people to get onto the next high speed train with a minimum of fuss, important for those returning to their home city after a work day in another city
- And most importantly, trains stations are located in the centre of cities, and airports are often located far from the city, and the travel time to and from the airport can be up to an hour, or in some cases even more, each way.

And to be fair, there are also disadvantages to high speed rain, and the most important one is cost. Air travel requires only two airports, and some radar stations, whereas high speed rail requires long tracks that must be maintained, and built. At a cost of anywhere from 15 to 50 million US per route kilometre (in 2012 dollars), the costs of hundreds of kilometres of track can very quickly become prohibitive.

High speed rail systems generate almost all of their revenue from ticket sales, and not from shops and shopping centres. High speed rail systems generally have very few stations, and the level of development of these stations may be low. Revenue is generated from ticket sales, so the trains need to have a high load factor (the load factor being the percentage of seats that are filled). Ticketing for high speed rail can get quite complicated, as it is possible to have discounts for early purchase, or group tickets, or passes that allow for multiple trips within a certain time period.

From a rail transportation planning perspective, high speed rail is relatively easy to plan. Very major cities are needed at each end of the rail line, as large numbers of passengers are needed to justify the expense of maintaining the system. The optimal distance for high speed rail is about 500 kms, but anywhere between 300 and 700 kms is also ok. The terrain needs to be fairly flat, and the presence of mountains will make things very difficult.

Long Distance Rail

One type of rail system that is often forgotten is the long distance rail system. This book uses this title for this type of rail system, but in truth there is no universally accepted definition for this type of system. This category applies for trains that travel over 5 or 6 hours to get to their destination, or even longer. In Australia the train trip from Sydney to Perth takes 3.5 days.

Long distance services are often overnight, and passengers sleep on them. More expensive tickets offer passengers a sleeper berth, and they may sleep in comfort on the train. The experience in Australia has been that sleeper berths are easily the most popular option for long distance rail, despite their additional cost, and are always booked out before other ticket classes.

Below is a photo of a travel compartment in a sleeper carriage in the long distance train that travels from Kuala Lumpur to Singapore. Long distance travel is still somewhat common in Malaysia, and sleepers are available on many night time trains. In a private room there are two bunk beds, as well as a toilet and shower.

Sleeper Compartment in Malaysia

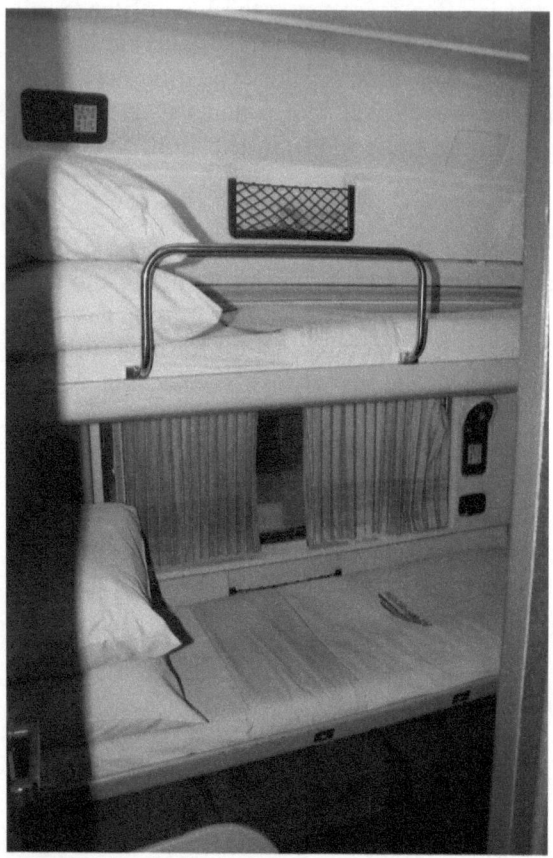

Long distance services are common in Australia, as the distances are so large. There are a number of train services where travel takes well over a day, and these trips can get very boring. The author's experience of this trips is that many of them are rather dull.

Where a rail line has not been upgraded to HSR, or even to a reasonable speed, then overnight distance trains are common. For passengers sleeping on the train makes the trip appear to pass faster, even though it is still a long trip. To justify having sleeper berths on trains, the travel time needs to be at least 7 hours, but preferably 9. Otherwise passengers will have an interrupted sleep, and arrive at their destination at an early time in the morning. For example, a train that leaves at 9pm, and takes 6 hours to reach its destination, will arrive at 3am in the morning. Unless passengers are allowed to stay and sleep in their beds then many will be unwilling to wake at this time in the morning.

Where the train trip is especially long, and the rail operator has made an attempt to upgrade the service, then sometimes the long distance trip is referred to as a rail cruise. A rail cruise can be extremely expensive, thousands of US dollars, and can be over 10 thousand US dollars for 2 people. A rail cruise is often slower than a normal long distance service, and may stop for a time in different cities, and provide tours to places of interest in the city. This kind of service is rare in Australia, but the small number of services provided are profitable, and it's a rare example of a rail company operator generating a healthy profit. In Australia a company called Great Southern Railways provides rail cruises that are very long, in some cases 21 days, and their trains travel all over Australia. These cruises, like everything in Australia, are very expensive, and are more similar to ocean cruises than rail a service.

Long distance overnight trains that offer sleeper berths seem to be disappearing, especially from Europe. Only a very small number of people can be moved in a sleeper carriage, in one sleeper carriage in Malaysia, the capacity of the carriage was 12 people, a very small number. Sleeper carriages are rarely economical to operate, and the cost to passengers to have a separate cabin with beds can be very high. The role and significance of overnight travel seems to be shrinking.

Other Rail Systems

Monorails

Monorails are normally classified as a type of rail system even though monorails systems are significantly different to almost all other rail systems. Monorails were a popular transport system in the 80's but have since fallen out of favour. There are many monorail systems installed in the world, and possibly the most significant is the commuter monorail system in Tokyo, which connects Haneda airport with the rest of Tokyo city. This monorail moves more people than any other monorail in the world per day. Kuala Lumpur also has a monorail line, which is very heavily used.

Maglev systems are a type of monorail, but are discussed separately below. Maglevs differ from monorails in the way the rail vehicle is propelled.

Mumbai in India is constructing a new monorail line, which, if the first line is successful, will be the start of a very large monorail system. Whilst monorail systems are still being built, they are mostly installed in airports, theme parks and other entertainment related venues, such as casinos and hotels. Serious commuter monorails are rare, and there may be only 20 in the entire world. Overall the experience with monorails has not been a happy one, and several monorails have been installed, only to be removed later. Bankruptcies and failed companies are common with monorail systems.

Monorails can perform very similarly to any other rail system. Rubber tyred monorails can climb grades of up to 6% and top speeds of 80 to 90 kms/hr seem common. Monorails are most comparable to intermediate capacity metros, as they travel at about the same speeds, and carry similar number of people. They also cost about the same amount of money per route kilometre. The system under construction in Mumbai has an estimated cost of only US $22 million per kilometre, which is a good price, but similar to what was paid for the Skytrain in Bangkok.

The picture below is of the Kuala Lumpur monorail. The vehicle length is rather low, but it is a very effective rail system and moves large numbers of people, despite its short length.

A Monorail in Kuala Lumpur

One criticism of monorails is that the monorail itself, what the monorail vehicle runs on, is unsightly. Another way of saying the same thing is to describe the monorail as visually intrusive. This is true, although not as visually intrusive as an intermediate capacity metro, built on an elevated system.

Monorails are really intermediate capacity systems. The capacity of a single monorail is unlikely to be more than 500 people, which is about the limit for light rail and intermediate capacity metros. Monorails currently are not able to carry thousands of people in one train, as a full metro can.

The high frequency of failure of monorails as a system is somewhat baffling. As a transport system they are safe, and cheap to build, and operate at reasonable speeds. It is surprisingly that monorails have been so unsuccessful in so many cases. Perhaps some reasons for the many failures of monorails are:
- Monorails compete with light rail and intermediate capacity metros, such as the DLR, or the Bangkok Skytrain, and do not quite perform as well
- Monorails cannot be expanded to have the same capacity as full metros
- Monorails cannot travel large distances, as most passengers stand when travelling on a monorail
- The ride quality in a monorail is not quite as good as light rail or metros
- Many monorail systems suffered from excessive political interference, especially during the planning stage
- Many monorails had a very low design capacity, and so were unlikely to ever generate a profit
- Transport orientated development is more difficult with elevated monorail stations, as they are smaller, reducing revenue
- Monorails have no real cost advantage compared to intermediate capacity metros
- Most importantly, a power failure for a monorail can have terrible consequences, as cranes need to be employed to remove trapped passengers, unlike intermediate capacity metros, where passengers can walk to the next station

On the other hand, some of the advantages of monorails are:
- Quick to build
- Cheap

- Monorails can accept sharp curves, down to as low as 50 metres (that said, light rail vehicles can accept 15 to 25 metre curves)
- The airspace needed for monorails is smaller than for light metros

Overall, one could easily say that monorails offer no real advantages over a light metro system, and have only disadvantages, the most important of which is the inability to get passengers off a train that breaks down. It would seem reasonable to recommend that monorail systems should only be used where light rail or an intermediate capacity metro is impossible, and this would generally be rare.

Maglevs

Perhaps one of the most interesting rail systems is a technology called the "Maglev". This technology has been in existence since the 80's and there is constant talk of the installation of new maglev systems. At the time of writing of this book only one commercial Maglev system is in operation, and this connects Pudong airport to the Shanghai metro system. A picture of this system is below:

Shanghai Maglev

Maglev stands for magnetic levitation, and the train itself does not have any wheels and does not even contact the monorail. The train floats above the monorail and, as it has no contact with the monorail, can reach speeds of over 400 kms/hr.

Maglev technology is very interesting because Maglev trains can reach such high speeds, but in practise only one commercial system has ever been installed. There also exists a low speed Maglev system in Japan, but its top speed is very low, so the full potential of the technology is not achieved.

The author is not convinced by the arguments for a maglev train. The major problem to be overcome is economics, and central to this is the cost of accelerating trains to speeds over 400 kms/hr. A number of high speed trains have been developped, using conventional tracks, where speeds of over 350 kms/hr have been achieved. These trains rarely operate over 300 kms/hr as the power consumption required to drive trains at any speed faster than that is very high. Power consumption seems to increase exponentially with speed, and at 400 kms/hr power consumption must be very large indeed. This problem cannot really be resolved, other than constructing a maglev tunnel with no air in it, something that seems rather improbable.

Tilt Trains

Tilt trains are an interesting type of technology used on intercity and regional services. The train tilts so that it can go around sharp curves at a higher speed. The speed increase can be considerable, and this technology, and the equations to calculate maximum speeds.

The greater the degree of tilt, the better the train can accept sharp curves. Tilt trains have revolutionised rail travel between many different centres, and can dramatically increase higher average speeds on existing rail lines, especially where those lines contain a lot of curves.

Tilt trains are normally only single deck, and passengers must be seated. The tilting action makes standing on a tilt train a little difficult.

The photo below is of a tilt train in Taiwan. It does not really appear any different to any other trains, although the outer shape is slightly different from other trains.

A Tilt Train in Taiwan

Tilting trains are usually regional or intercity trains, that travel from one city to another. It would be strange to use a tilt train within one large city, as a substitute for a metro or commuter system.

Tourist Trains

A tourist train is a train which provides an enjoyable experience to passengers, and may or may not connect important destinations that passengers may want to go. Most tourist railways go nowhere important, and the experience is the reason why the service is popular. Alternatively, a tourist railway may connect tourist destinations to the main rail system.

Tourist railways often use old rollingstock, which is custom made for that particular application. The structure of the rollingstock may be very unusual, and may not even afford protection from rain or wind.

Some tourist railways connect hard to reach places, and the rollingstock required to achieve this can be very distinctive.

The picture below shows two different types of tourist tram in the town of Christchurch in New Zealand. On the left is the tourist tram that runs around the city, which is an old style tram that is rigid and very short. On the right is a tram that has been converted to be used as a restaurant.

Tourist Trams in Christchurch

Tourist railways can be divided into several categories:
- Railways through parklands, mountains, and other areas which are very scenic and the entire trip might last 1 to 2 hours. The Kuranda railway form Cairns in Australia up into the nearby mountains is probably the best known example of this type of train in Australia, but there are several others.
- Rail cruises, where the rail trip might take weeks, or in some cases, months. The cost of the ticket is extremely high, potentially thousands or tens of thousands of US dollars, for one ticket. Food is provided, and the quality can be very high. Passengers will sleep on the train. The Indian Pacific in Australia is an example of this type of rail service.
- Trains that are mostly "normal", but are richly decorated, and connect the rail system to an area which tourists commonly visit. The commuter train in Paris to the palace at Versailles is

a good example of this kind of train, other examples include the Disneyland train in Hong Kong, or the Xinbeitou train in Taipei to the hots springs resorts. These trains are often visually impressive and richly appointed. There are no trains like this in Australia
- Old heritage trams that move throughout cities. These trams are often 100 years old, and have a lot of charm. The distance moved might be quite small. The best known example of this type of tram is the San Francisco heritage tram.
- Trains, that are more like trolleys, that climb steep inclines, and connect major destinations to carparks or other access points to a high value destination. This type of tourist railway is relatively common, and Perhaps the best known of these is the Peak Tram in Hong Kong, which connects the Peak on Hong Kong Island with the rest of the island. This type of tourist railway is sometimes used to connect mountains and ski fields to access points.
- Small railways, sometimes monorails, contained entirely in amusement parks, and are paid for an operated by the amusement park owner.

As can be seen from the list above, tourist railways are actually quite common and varied.

Tourist trains have high ticket prices, and so can operate at a profit. Passengers rarely would use a tourist railway for daily transportation.

REFERNCES

1. Zhang, Y & Yan, X & Comtois, C *Some Measures of Increasing Rail Transit Riderships: Case Studies*, Chinese Geographical Science, Volume 10, Number 1, pp 80 – 88, 2000

2. Smith K. *Alstom puts weight behind Citadis Dualis*, International Railway Journal, Feb 2010

3. ALSTOM, *AGV Full Speed Ahead into the 21st Century*, 2009, www.transport.alstom.com

4. BTS Group, *Annual Report 2009/2010* (the Bangkok Skytrain)

5. Kemp, R. *T618 – Traction Energy Metrics*, Rail Safety and Standards Board, Interfleet Technology, Dec 2007

6. Taipei Rapid Transit Corporation *2013 Annual Report*, http://english.metro.taipei/ct.asp?xItem=1056448&ctNode=70219&mp=122036

7. Dearien, J. *Ultralight Rail and Energy Use*, Encyclopaedia of Energy, Elsevier Publishing, March 2004

8. Siemens, *Siemens Velaro datasheet*, www.siemens.com/mobility

9. Fabian, J. *The Exceptional Service of Driverless Metros*, Journal of Advanced Transportation, Vol 33, No 1, pp 5-16

10. Kimijima, N. et al *New Urban Transport for Middle East Monorail System for Dubai Palm Jumeirah Transit System*, Hitachi Review Vol 59, (2010), No 1

11. IBI Group, E&N Railway Corridor Study: Analysis of Tourist Train Potential, (Date Unknown)

12. Hassan A The Role of Light Railway in Sugarcane Transport in Egypt, Infrastructure Design, Signalling and Security in Railway, Chapter 1

13. Parsons Brinkerhoff *High Speed Rail*, Network, Issue No 73, Sept 2011, http://www.pbworld.com/news/publications.aspx

14. Chun-Hwan, K. Transportation Revolution: The Korean High-speed Railway, Japan Railway & Transport Review 40, March 2005

15. Alstom Metropolis 21 st Century Metro Train Technology, http://www.alstom.com/turkey/products-and-services/-alstom-transport-turkey/rolling-stock/

16. Scomi Rail, *Monorail The Revolution of Urban Transit*, http://www.scomirail.com.my/

17. Duncan, B *The Hunter Rail Car: A versatile design solution for regional rail transport*, Australian Journal of Multi-disciplinary Engineering, Vol 7, No 2

18. Burge, P. et al Modelling Demand for Long-Distance Travel in Great Britain, www.rand.org, 2011

19. Railway Gazette *Commissioning the world's heaviest automated metro*, Metro Report 2003

20. Stadler *Electric Double-Deck train KISS*, www.stadlerrail.com

21. Transportation Research Board *Integration of Light Rail Transit into City Streets*, 1996

22. Turnbull, G. *The development and retention of Melbourne's trams and the influence of Sir Robert Risson*, ISSN 1038-7448, Working Paper No. 01/2002, Aug 2002

23. Transportation Research Board *Track Design Handbook for Light Rail Transit*, Second Edition, TCRP Report 155, 2012

24. Mora, J. *A Streetcar named Light Rail*, IEEE Spectrum Feb 1991

25. Sarunac, R. & Zeolla, N. *Structural and Crashworthiness Requirements of Light Rail Vehicles with Low-Floor Extension*, Transportation Research Circular E-C058: 9th National Light Rail Conference

26. Schroeder, M. *Developing CEM Design Standards to Improve Light Rail Vehicle Crashworthiness*, Proceedings of JRC2006 Joint Rail Conference April 2006 Atlanta

27. Daniel, L. *Light Rail Systems – Assessing Technical Feasibility*, Conference on Railway Engineering Melbourne May 2006

28. Swanson, J. & Thomes, C. *Light-Rail Transit Systems*, IEEE Vehicular Technology Magazine, June 2010

29. Transportation Research Board National Research Council *TCRP Report 2 Applicability of Low-Floor Light Rail Vehicles in North America*, 1995

30. Coifman, B. *IVHS protection at light rail grade crossings*, Proceedings of the 1995 IEEE/ASME Joint Railroad Conference, 1995

31. Swanson, J. *Light Rail Systems Without Wires*, Proceedings of the 2003 IEEE/ASME Joint Rail Conference April 2003

32. Maunsell Australia Pty Ltd, *Perth Light Rail Study*, 0284/05, August 2007

Chapter 4 A Very Basic Introduction to Rail Infrastructure

Rail infrastructure is a very large topic, and this chapter is no more than a very short review of the key infrastructure items that are relevant to station design. Platform gaps are affected by the track system, and platform gaps are very important for the design of any station. Platform gaps are reduced for concrete slab track. One of the advantages of tram systems is the use of rail tracks embedded into a road, which allows platforms to be very close to train edges when trains enter a station.

Tunnel design and configuration can also affect stations. Tunnel design results in a choice of either side of island platforms, which we will see is a very important choice. Island platforms are considered superior to side platforms, and look and feel better for passengers. Side platforms are difficult to install for certain types of tunnel configuration.

Track

Most rail systems use a fairly standard track system, with the exception of trams, monorails, and some light rail. For trams the rails are often embedded into the road, so as to allow road vehicles to pass over the rails as well as trams. Rails for trams have a separate and quite different design to normal rail. The shape of the rail, as well as the system by which the rail is held in place, is quite different.

Rails are made of steel. Some smaller rail systems run on concrete viaducts, but the vast majority of rail systems use steel rails. Train wheels are also often made of steel, and the behaviour of this steel to steel physical interface is very important. Surprisingly, the steel wheels of the train can often slide over the steel top surface, and when this happens the top of the rail and the wheel can be badly damaged. Care must be taken in ensuring that the wheel never slides over the rail, but rolls instead, and this requirement is central to the design of any rail system. One way to avoid this problem is to use rubber tyred trains, and this is occasionally done, such as the Montreal metro, but so doing adds a lot of cost as rubber tyres need to be constantly replaced as they wear.

Much of the track around the world is ballasted, which means the sleepers and rails sit on ballast. Ballast is made up of crushed rock, and major railways use substantial quantities of it. Sleepers sit within the ballast, and the ballast holds them in place. The major alternative to ballasted track is slab track, where the sleepers and rail sit directly on concrete. The track structure for ballasted track is shown below.

Figure 4.1 Track System

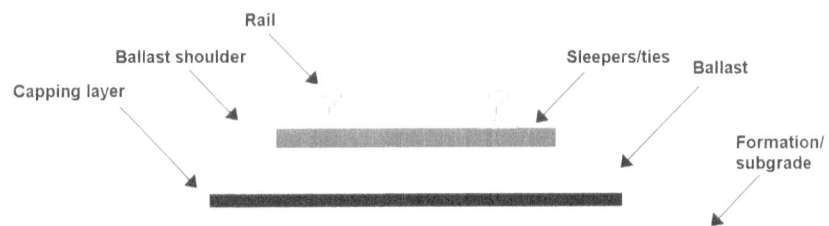

The function of each of the components of the track system is:
- The rail; supports the train, provides a running surface for the wheels of each train.
- Sleepers; which support the rails, hold the rails at a fixed distance from each other, and transfer the weight and load of the train into the ballast. Sleepers are often made of wood or concrete, although other materials such as steel or polymer are also used
- Ballast, which sits under the rails, and is made of hard crushed rock. Ballast distributes the load from trains, reducing wear, so that many trains can pass which serious damage to the track system. Ballast is a sacrificial item, which means it is designed to degrade over time. The degradation of ballast, and managing its replacement, is one of the key maintenance activities of any railway.
- The capping layer; which provides separation between the ballast and the subgrade. The capping layer maintains the separation between the ballast and the formation. The capping layer is sometimes replaced with geosynthetics, which is a type of textile matting, keeping the formation and ballast separate.
- Formation: which is usually the compacted ground underneath the track structure. The formation supports the track, and the condition of the formation is one of the key parameters for determining the maintenance of track.

Tracks are normally in pairs. Away from the track the ground normally has a fall to it, this is to allow for the water to run away from the track.

Figure 4.2 The Double Track System

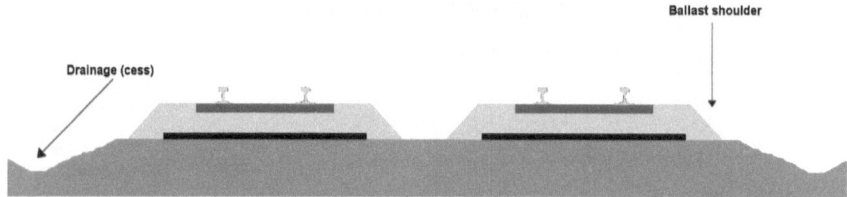

Drainage is very important for any track system. Drains need to be provided so that water can be removed when the track is rained on. Drainage, or the lack of it, can cause substantial problems in any rail system.

The rails are fastened to the sleepers with specially designed fasteners. The picture below shows the clips holding the rails to the sleepers.

Rail Track

If the reader looks carefully, it can be noticed that most of the rail is rusty, but on top of the rail there is part of it where train wheels sit when travelling over the rail. This patch of worn shiny rail is called the wear band, or the contact band, and it's important for a rail system to maintain this clear band of clean steel for signalling equipment to operate. The picture below shows it better.

Rail Fastenings

Rails are quite standard, and come in a number of sizes. Rail sizes are usually expressed in weight per unit of length, and in metric countries this is often 53 or 60 kgs per metre. Other sizes are also possible, with 40 and 50 also being common. In the large heavy haul freight networks in northern Australia, 74 kg/metre is now being used, which is a very large size and suitable for very heavily loaded trains with a high frequency. The imperial unit of measurement is pounds per yard, and 40 to 100 pounds per yard is common.

Increasing the size of the rail increases the size of train that can pass over the rails. For a light rail system, only a small rail is needed, and where small trains are then only small rails are needed. For larger trains, and especially freight lines, the rails need to be large to accommodate the higher weight.

Figure 4.3 The Rail Profile

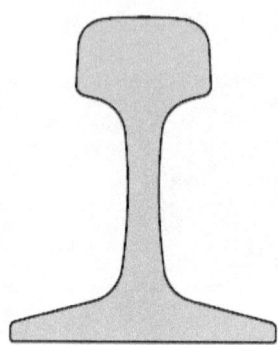

Above is a very standard profile for rails. The top is called the head of the rail. Different sizes of rail have slightly different shapes, but overall they mostly look similar to the rail shape above. Tram rails look significantly different, and monorails do not have rails, but just the one beam. The image below shows the profile of a tram rail, and it is designed to allow trains to run on it and allow road vehicles to drive over it as well.

Figure 4.4 Tram Rail Profile

The ballast underneath the track is really important. The main purpose of ballast is to maintain and support the track, which is generally does well, but also to suppress vibration. Trains moving over tracks generate a lot of noise and vibration, and the ballast, surprisingly enough, suppresses this. Ballast is even used in tunnels, to suppress noise, which is does quite well. It seems strange that ballast does this, but it does.

Ballast is made up of many small hard rocks. The amount of ballast placed under the track is not fixed, and more is usually better. Putting more ballast is expensive, as the stuff is unexpectedly expensive, and actually quite heavy. The best ballast if tough and rough, and locks together to form a really tight bed for the sleepers and rails. Generally the harder the better, and quartz and granite are often considered the best materials, but many different types of rock are used. Railways often use materials that are found locally, to reduce costs and ensure the ballast does not need to be shipped very far.

Achieving the great noise reduction that ballast achieves is done through breaking down the ballast. Each time a train passes over the ballast, a small amount of it breaks into smaller pieces. Over a long period of time, such as decades, the ballast breaks down into such small pieces that most of it becomes powder. The powder intermixed with the rocky ballast is often described as fines. Once the ballast is full of fines it needs to be either cleaned, or entirely replaced, and both of these options are not cheap. Also, the track will be unable to hold track geometry, and this can be a real problem for high speed track where maintaining good track geometry is quite important.

So in summary ballast is a sacrificial item. This means that it is designed to be destroyed, which on most tracks it will be sooner or later. As ballast degrades, it gets smaller, and so the track starts to sink. Over a period of time the track can sink up to 200 mm, and if this occurs at a platform, train floors will be lower than the platform. Alternatively, railways often top up ballast as it degrades.

Ballast and maintaining it drives a very large part of the maintenance for a rail system. There is much to be said about what type of ballast to install, when to clean it, and when to replace it. These decisions are important for the maintenance of a rail system, and a good rail maintenance organisation will carefully consider how to make these decisions. For the purposes of rail transport planning, the choice of ballast, or even if it is to be used, can influence the way services are provided to customers. This very detailed and interesting topic is unfortunately a bit too long to be fully explained here; one of the many compromises needed to complete this book and not let it get too long. But to provide a very quick summary:

- Better quality ballast costs more, and degrades more slowly. Reducing the maintenance can sometimes mean spending more on the ballast when it is purchased
- Better quality ballast provides more track stability and the geometry degrades more slowly
- Providing more ballast when the track is installed, or deeper ballast, allows the load from trains to be spread more evenly and the ballast will degrade more slowly. An alternative is to use lighter trains, or a lower frequency of service
- The geometry requirements for high speed rail are very high, and so using ballast means that track geometry will need to be constantly checked

Below is a very simple explanation of how ballast degrades and its effect on track geometry. The diagram below looks at track side on, so we can see what happens when ballast degrades.

Figure 4.5 Track in Good Condition

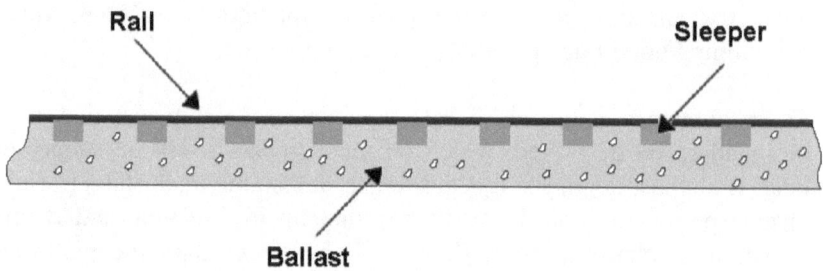

The track above is nice and flat and will provide a lovely smooth running surface for trains. Once the track has been used for a few years, and depending on a few things like the type of traffic, how much of it there is, and the amount of rainfall and the quality of the drainage, then the track will start to sink. When it sinks then it will start to look something like what is drawn below:

Figure 4.6 Degraded Track

Again, the overall mechanics of track degradation have been heavily simplified here. There are a number of other track geometry parameters, and these also degrade, and need to be checked and measured by qualified maintenance personnel. Despite this, what is shown above is the most common cause of track geometry problems, and the one that usually determines much of the maintenance spending.

The degradation of ballast is a real problem for station design. It needs to be accounted for, and the track and rail position "moves around". This presents many problems, the most important of which, is that the platform gap needs to be increased in size. In some cases the platform gap is enormous, and this can be a real problem for people with disabilities.

The photo below is of tram tracks in Hong Kong that have been uncovered during maintenance work. Rarely is there any ballast for tram tracks, and as can be seen from the photo below the tracks are embedded into the road, and surrounded in bitumen. This type of systems does not allow the noise suppression that normally comes with using ballast, especially at joins, ie, where two rails are joined together.

Uncovered Tram Tracks in Hong Kong

So why is more slab track not used? Slab track, or putting the rails and sleepers onto concrete, seems to eliminate many of the problems associated with ballast. Ballast is expensive, and needs to be replaced after it has degraded. When it sinks it creates all sorts of track geometry problems, which can only be fixed with expensive track maintenance vehicles.

Slab track in Bangkok is shown below, on the Bangkok Skytrain. Note that on this track a third rail is also used, and it is located in between both running tracks.

Slab Track in Bangkok

Slab track is technically more complex to install. Problems with vibration usually mean that the concrete base can be damaged, and so vibration damping is needed. Whilst this function is normally provided by ballast, this is not possible with slab track, so some complicated vibration dampening scheme is needed. Different types of these have been designed and are in use, and quality control when they are installed is very important.

Tunnels

The design and structure of tunnels will often determine the type of underground station. Consequently it is important for station design to understand the type of tunnel, as this will determine the station configuration.

Tunnelling is a challenging area of engineering. The soil conditions are important to the costs and challenges associated with tunnelling, and there is no real way to know what the soil conditions will be like without actually tunnelling. To get an appreciation of the ground conditions, a project may organise for test bores to be drilled to sample what the ground is like, and this will provide some information on what the ground conditions are like. Whilst test bores provide some information, the actual ground conditions won't be known until digging actually commences.

Tunnels, and the management of fire in a tunnel, will impact upon station design. A "standard" tunnel will have ventilation, although many do not. All the ventilation equipment will normally be located at a station. An underground station can have a large amount of equipment, located in several large rooms within the station. The need to ventilate a tunnel significantly adds to the cost of constructing an underground station.

The picture below shows a rail tunnel, with the photo taken from one end of an underground station. Rail tunnels are commonly black or very dark with not much lighting. In this case this tunnel is single bore, and the track is ballasted, rather that being slab track. Note that the lighting is very close to the floor of the tunnel, so that drivers won't experience flashing lights when passing them, something that in rare instances can cause epileptic seizures.

A Tunnel and Portal

Whilst underground stations are also strictly speaking tunnels, they are not referred to as such, and the tunnels actually connect two underground stations. The transition from station to tunnel is shown below, with the station being light coloured and well-lit, and the tunnel dark and black. The transition from station into a tunnel is called a portal.

Rail tunnels can be described in terms of the following:
- The length of the tunnel
- What type of traffic is permitted to move through the tunnel
- The diameter of the tunnel, or if not round, the cross-sectional area
- The type of ventilation
- If the tunnel is single bore or double bore, and the configuration. These are discussed in depth below

So let's discuss each of these in turn.

The length of the tunnel is probably the most important parameter for any rail tunnel. Usually measured in metres, it is measured as a distance that a person following the rail track would walk, rather than a linear distance from one portal to another. A long tunnel would be over 1 km in length, although there are many tunnels over 10kms, these are a small percentage of the total number of tunnels worldwide. In the US tunnels less than 160 metres are not described as tunnels, and are not normally classified as tunnels (at least under NFPA 130).

Most rail tunnels have passenger traffic moving through them. The composition of the rail traffic is quite important for a rail tunnel, but a casual observer would probably not be able to tell from looking at the tunnel what type of traffic was using the tunnel. Putting either diesel freight or passenger trains through the tunnel may change the equipment installed into it, or maybe not. Most freight trains are diesel powered, and this fuel is carried on board the train, and fuel leaks and fires are possible. Diesel engines can also catch fire, and this is particularly the case with older or more poorly maintained locomotives. Diesel locomotives dramatically increase the risk in a tunnel, and so it is very important for the rail planner to know if freight will be moving through the tunnel.

The risk and challenge with rail tunnels is fires. As tunnels are confined spaces, any fires can quickly kill any passengers in the train. The heat itself is not the danger, but the smoke produced from the fire. Small fires are often started through vandalism in trains, but large fires are rare. The hazard of a large fire has a very low probability of occurrence, but when they occur the number of deaths can be very large. Preventing fires, or providing some method of escape for a tunnel can greatly add to the cost of the construction of a rail tunnel, so it is important for the planner to know how this safety risk should be managed. This topic is discussed extensively in chapter 19.

The diameter of the tunnel is an important measure. Most tunnels are roughly circular in shape, so it's possible to calculate the cross-sectional area of the tunnel from the diameter, using the very simple formula $Area = \dfrac{\pi D^2}{4}$. A typical diameter for a rail tunnel is about 7 metres, and a typical cross-sectional area about 40 to 60 metres. Larger cross sectional areas make ventilation and management of the movement of air in the tunnel easier, and overall a larger tunnel is better than a smaller one. Trains need to push the air out of the way when moving through a tunnel, and where there is little room between the walls of the tunnel and the train then the power needed to move the train is significantly greater. Also very narrow tunnels will make the air hotter as trains pass through, and the heat can become very great.

The type of ventilation is also very important, and there are a number of different types. Many tunnels have no ventilation at all, but for new tunnels ventilation is often installed. Ventilation is required based on the length of the tunnel, the frequency of traffic, and the cross-sectional area of the tunnel. Ventilation can be described as either transverse, or longitudinal. For transverse ventilation air is pushed into the tunnel from the walls towards the middle of the tunnel, whereas longitudinal the air is pushed in from the end of the tunnel, from one end to another. The key question for the rail planner is whether ventilation is needed at all, and as with many tunnel systems, it is much cheaper to not install than install it.

And the final part of describing a rail tunnel is its configuration, and if it is single or twin bore. The table below lists many of the different configurations possible for a rail tunnel.

Different Tunnel Configurations	
Tunnel Type	Comment
	This is a single cut and cover tunnel. Cut and cover tunnels often have straight

Introduction to Rail Infrastructure   Page 72

Different Tunnel Configurations

Tunnel Type	Comment
	sides, unlike the curved sides of the other tunnels below. As cut and cover tunnels are often close to the surface, ventilation is often easy, and so double bore cut and cover tunnels are rare.
	This is a tunnel with two tracks, in a single bore tunnel. There is no separate tunnel for escape or for service vehicles. The shape of the upper tunnel is often described as a horseshoe.
	A tunnel with two tracks, with a circular tunnel. There is no separate escape or service tunnel. This type of tunnel is common in deeply bored tunnels.
	A circular rail tunnel with a supporting rail passage. This configuration is helpful if the need arises for an escape from the tunnel, and getting maintenance staff to equipment in the tunnel.

Different Tunnel Configurations

Tunnel Type	Comment
	The additional tunnel is expensive to construct.
	A horseshoe shaped tunnel, with a large concrete wall down the middle. The tunnel is split into two sections, which allows passengers to escape should the need arise down one of the two tunnels. This tunnel construction is commonly used in Hong Kong, and is relatively cheap.
	A double bore tunnel with cross-passages between each of the tunnels. This kind of configuration is common for long tunnels and those that carry freight.
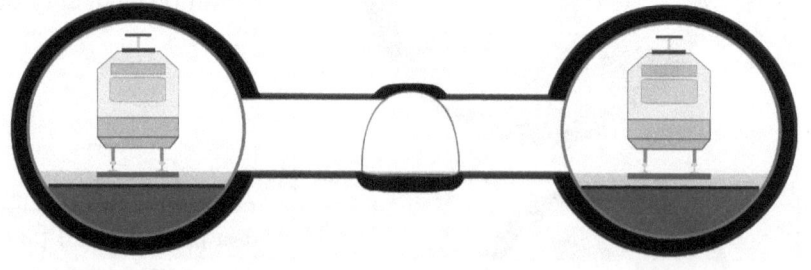	A double bore tunnel with a service tunnel in the middle, with cross passages. This is the configuration used on the Chunnel between England and France. This configuration is a very good one, and convenient for maintenance and escape from fires. Unfortunately it's really expensive.

Below is the layout of a twin bore tunnel in plan view. The key features are shown.

Figure 4.7 Rail Track through Tunnels

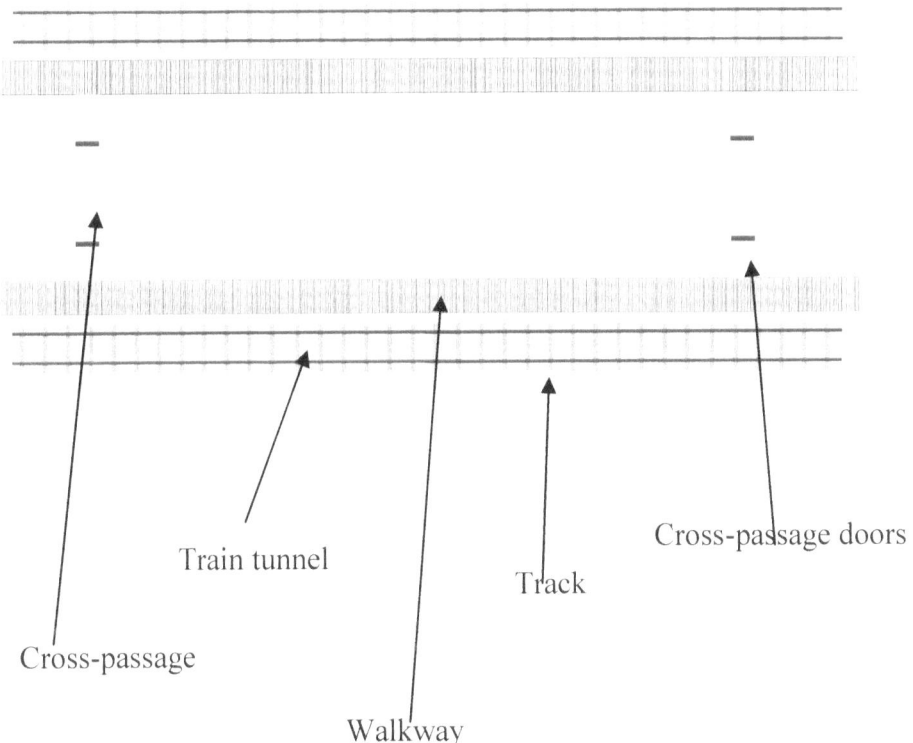

The main components of this tunnel system are:
1/ the tunnels
2/ the tracks
3/ the walkway next to the tracks
4/ the cross-passages
5/ the doors in the cross-passages.

For station design, we note that rail tunnels are with the two tracks side by side are normally built with side platforms, and those with twin tunnels are island platforms. Will this rule does not need to always be followed, it often is.

Chapter 5 Basic Station Types

We start our discussion of station design with identifying a number of key features of stations. One a station is constructed then changing its configuration is almost impossible. Whilst equipment can be added and removed, changes to configuration are very difficult to make. Station configuration also has a powerful effect on the way the station interacts with the rest of the network. The choice of station configuration is an important one.

Styles and Configurations of Stations

Stations come in a large array of different configurations. Stations can be described in terms of a number of simple parameters, which are commonly understood throughout the rail industry. Some of these are:

- Platform length. Typically platforms are raised and higher than both the ground and the track running alongside it, and the length of the platform is same as the length of the train that can sit alongside it, and passengers can board and disembark safely. Not all platforms however are the same length as the trains that stop there.
- Height of the platform. This measurement is taken from the top of the running surface of the rail to the place where passengers stand to board a train.
- Number of platforms. Each platform typically will have a separate track alongside it, although in some cases a very long platform may be classified as two separate platforms.
- Number of passengers through the station each day. Almost always the number of passengers is counted through the ticketing system, and the number of barrier/gate entries and exits is counted per day.
- The role the station plays in the operation of the network. Stations may be very large and play an important role in the network or small and trains may stop there only rarely. Some stations are used only for special events. Alternatively, a station can be a terminus, where services terminate and do not continue, or am interchangestation, where passengers can alight from one service on one rail line, and then board a service on another line.

- If the station is underground, at the same grade as the ground, or elevated. These differences are important for the design and use of the station.

Some stations may have disused platforms, and these are not normally counted as part of the total number of platforms. Old stations may have a substantial number of disused platforms, and the numbering or identification of platforms may reflect this. At Rockdale station in Sydney platform numbering runs from 2 to 5, as platform 1 is no longer used, and the platform numbers have not changed since that platform was built over 50 years ago.

The station below is typical of stations in remote areas, and there is only one track at this platform. Trains moving in both directions stop at the same platform. There is no track on the other side. Also note that the station has no roofing, although there is a small area provided, a bit like a shed, where passengers can stand to get out of the rain. Stations of this kind are rarely manned with staff, as there is no booking office for staff to sell tickets at, or store cleaning implements, or any of the other accessories of an office.

A Simple Regional Station

This station has only one track, which has some advantages and disadvantages. A carpark on the side of the station without a track may be accessed without crossing any tracks, which for disabled passengers

Basic Station Types Page 77

is a real benefit. Alternatively, the number of trains that can pass through this station will be limited to a small number per hour, as trains moving in both directions will need to pass over the same track. Another configuration possible with thinly used stations is that there ia a loop around the station, allowing trains top stop at both platforms to pass one another.

We can see the facilities provided on this station, which is in outer Sydney. There is no booking office, so no staff will ordinarily be present to help passengers and sell tickets. Seating and lighting is provided, as well as a covered waiting area. The covered area will provide some protection from rain, but given its small size will provide shelter for only maybe 20 passengers, and no more. There are no vending machines, nor any screens providing information on when the next train is due. There are no barriers to restrict entry to the station, and passengers can move around freely. The reader may notice a small yellow box under the orange sign attached to the waiting area, which is a help point for any passengers who feel their safety is threatened. There are no lifts or escalators of any kind.

Whilst this particular station is in a remote area of Sydney, this configuration of station is very common in Australia. There are hundreds of this type of basic yet functional station across the country, and these exist in all states of Australia. They are cheap to construct, and maintain, and perform an important function whilst being relatively immune to damage from vandalism and weather. It may be that some transport planners feel that this type of station is somehow inadequate, but it is an efficient design that performs its function well.

The picture below is of a regional station outside of Paris. We may observe that this station has a clock, covered waiting areas, and is very long indeed. The platform height is also quite low, consistent with the platform heights across Europe and France especially. On the right hand side is a booking office, where tickets are sold, station staff work, and there is an air-conditioned office. Notice that the station has roofing over part of its length. Also notice that the two platforms are on the side of the track, and this configuration is called a side platform station. There is no obvious platform numbering on the station. Given that there is a waiting area and booking office on one side of the station, and not the other, this station is likely to be a commuter station, which passengers waiting to go to the city centre on one side, and using the other platform to only alight when returning from the nearby city (in this case Paris). This configuration is very common.

A Regional Station in Paris, Side Platforms

The station below is in urban Sydney, and is an island platform station. For this type of station the platforms are in the centre of the tracks, and trains move around the platforms. Passengers wait in the middle of the platform, and can wait in the same place for trains in either direction. Notice on this station there is a vending machine for Coke Cola drinks next to the wall of the old building in the middle of the platform. Express services bypass this station, and local all stopping services, which are slower, stop here with a low frequency.

A Suburban Station in Sydney, Island Platform

Island platforms are often considered superior to side platform stations. This is because:
- Rail staff can be placed in the middle of the island platform, to provide customer information, assistance, and sell tickets
- Toilets, if provided, need only to be located in the middle of the island platform
- In underground systems, island platforms are generally bigger, so there is more room for passengers to wait. For above ground stations with side platforms can be any size based on the nearby available land
- It obvious where passengers should wait, but with side platforms passengers need to make a decision.

There are also some disadvantages to island platforms, and some of these are:
- Island platforms often need more space, and this can particularly be a problem with elevated railways where space is quite limited
- Island platforms require tracks to move in a curve around the station. Notice in the pictures above that the tracks for the side platforms are very straight, whereas one of the tracks for the island platform needs to curve around the platform. If there are

high speed trains not stopping at the station this could be a real problem.
- Side platforms can be convenient for passengers with disabilities, as they can enter one platform directly from the carpark. This can be very handy as there is no need to use a lift, assuming that the platform is on the side for trains going in the desired direction
- Island platforms are more expensive than smaller side platforms, especially in underground stations

Another type of station is one where passengers need to request the train to stop, to either board or alight. For heavy rail these stations are relatively uncommon, but for light rail are extremely common. For tram systems this is normal, and the waiting passenger would signal the driver to stop, usually with a movement of a hand. In the US this kind of station is called a halt. There are also a small number of stations like this in Sydney. The stations above are not halts, which are never installed in busy city railways, but are always located in remote areas with very limited numbers of passengers.

Stations for tram systems tend to be very simple, likewise for classical "light rail" systems. Tram stations are mostly called stops, and are in most cases not really stations. Many of the stops are so small that that are almost invisible, and are can only be detected by a small street sign indicating that trams stop there. In some cases passengers may even need to board and alight from the side of the road to the waiting tram.

The photo below is a tram stop in Zurich. It is very basic, and there is an oval building alongside the tram tracks, which has a small number of shops in it. Note that the tram stop is just a flat space with no cover, no obvious lighting, and very little by way of facilities. This is common for tram stops, even in very busy cities.

A Tram Stop in Zurich

The photo below is a light rail station in Hong Kong. Light rail vehicles use this station to move passengers from the main metro line to apartment buildings in outer Hong Kong. From this photo we note that the platforms are quite high from the passenger walking surface to the top of the rail. Older light rail systems had this design, but this is now uncommon. Also note that the entire station is covered, but very poorly lit, and the platforms are very short. The photo was taken when standing on the tracks, something that is allowed with light rail and trams, but not with heavy rail. This station is a blend of a heavy rail station and a tram stop.

A Light Rail Station

Terminal Stations

Large terminal stations are places where regional, high speed and commuter trains meet and sit to allow passengers to change from one train to another. This type of central city station is quite common, and in the US and Canada these stations are often called "Union" station. There are union stations in Chicago, Los Angeles, Toronto, and Montreal, and many others. The most famous terminal station in the world is Grand Central Station in New York. In large cities there might be many terminal stations, for example, in Paris there are six. In all Australian cities there is only one in each major city.

Below is an example of a small terminal station. This one is in Perth. Services leave here for some regional destinations, and almost all commuter trains pass through this station. The high ceiling provides a feeling of space. Notice the platforms are numbered, and there are text passenger information displays for each platform. As is common with terminal station, trains are waiting for their scheduled departure times at the station.

Perth Main Station

Terminal stations often have flashy designs to make them look more impressive. Open areas to give a feeling of space and to make the station look sexy and more cool. Large open areas are common in large stations, although there is no real reason why all stations should not be designed in this way.

Major Components of a Station

Platform screen doors have become increasing common around the world. They are often installed in metro stations or at stations where there is significant crowding. To work properly the doors on the station need to line up with the doors on the train, and this is usually only possible with ATO (automatic train operation), where a computer drives the train. A human driver will rarely be accurate enough to allow a rail system to use platform screen doors.

Overall platform screen doors seem to be becoming more common, especially in Asia. Below is a picture of some platform screen doors in Singapore, and as with just about everything in Singapore, it's very clean and shiny. The platform screen doors below are full height, and completely the station from the tunnel in which the train moves.

Platform Screen Doors

Platform screen doors have a number of benefits, including:
- It is very difficult for people to commit suicide at stations with platform screen doors
- No one will be pushed under a train from overcrowding with platform screen doors
- The air-conditioning load for the station will be lower, as the air from the station will not mix with outside air
- The station looks better, as passengers cannot see the dirty tracks and tunnel, but instead see the clean shiny platform screen doors.

Of course no discussion of any asset in a rail system would be complete without mentioning the disadvantages:
- They are expensive
- They can fail, and this can delay trains
- Their use is limited to trains that are at least partially compute controlled, as drivers cannot stop their trains with the accuracy needed to position the train next to the platform doors.

Notice on the floors the lines painted to direct passengers. These are common in major metro lines where the number of passengers is very large. Passengers alighting move through the middle of the doors, and on the outsides wait for passengers to alight before boarding the train.

The doors above are full height doors, but it is not necessary to do that. Below is a picture of some half height doors in Tokyo, which provides many of the benefits of full length doors. In terms of passenger flow and safety the half height doors work quite well, but do not assist with air conditioning. Also note the advertising screens on the walls across from the platform.

Platform Edge Barriers

Concourses are the area above or near a station where many of the entrances and exists are connected. Passengers move throughout a station from the concourse, and it is often above the station. The photo below is of a metro station in Hong Kong. Long concourses like this are common in underground metro stations, where the station has the additional purpose of allowing people to move around the city without catching a train. In the front of the picture are the barriers that provide entry into the station proper, and on the left is a walkway to the other end of the station. The concourse here is above the platforms where the metro stations stop, and as the metro trains are quite long, the concourse also is quite long. The area behind the barriers is often referred to as the "paid area", where passengers need to buy a ticket to enter.

A Metro Station Concourse

Some of the stations in Hong Kong serve as major thoroughfares without the need for passengers to catch a train. Stations may be connected through overpasses, and passengers can walk along these to get to the next station without riding a train. In some cases pedestrian overpasses or shopping centres can extend for several kilometres, connecting several stations together.

The picture below is of a station in Osaka where the platforms are on both sides of the train, and doors are opened simultaneously on both sides of the train. In practice passengers enter form one side and exit from the other. This type of station is sometimes called the Spanish solution, because it is commonly used in the Barcelona metro. Passengers get on through one side of the train, and alight from the other. This structure of station is able to move more people quickly.

Barcelona Style Platforms for a Terminus Station in Osaka

The station structure above is sometimes used in terminus stations, and in stations with very high numbers of passengers. This station structure can be very effective in reducing dwell times.

Access in and out of Stations

Trains are large, and in many cases there are two or more tracks making up any rail line. Passengers need to be able to get from outside the rail corridor to the platform to catch a train. This means that need in many cases to either go over the top of below where a train might go, and where the train is quite large then going over the train requires passenger to climb quite a height.

The raised section over a station is called the concourse. For a station on flat ground, a concourse is quite common, and often stairs lead to the concourse from both outside the station, and from platforms.

The design below is a very good one, and there is no need for a concourse. For a side platform, where there are no barriers, this solution is quite acceptable, and there are only two ramps at this station, one in view and the other to the left. The ramp allows passengers to get across the tracks without getting in the path of trains. Also the ramp allows wheelchair passengers access across the tracks, without the need for a ramp.

A Station Ramp

Ramps are a cheap solution to providing access to stations for those with disabilities. Ramps also are very unlikely to fail, and require very little maintenance, unlike lifts and escalators.

There are international and national standards on ramp design. Normally ramps must be design to be below a certain grade, and a steep ramp will be difficult to those with disabilities to use. Also, long ramps need to have landings, which is a flat space where people with wheelchairs can rest during the ascent of a ramp.

Lifts can be used to get passengers from one platform to another, and from one side of the station to the other. Lifts are very popular with passengers, and will be extensively used where installed. Lifts will be unable to move large numbers of passengers, as they are too slow, but can be very effective in moving passengers with prams, disabilities, and those with luggage. Whilst expensive, the installation of lifts has become commonplace across Australia, even for regional stations.

A Station Lift

Mobility aids are a very important topic with stations. Adding mechanical aids to a station will help disabled people use the station more effectively, but they can be very expensive to install. On the left is a lift which can move people from the concourse to the platform. This type of free standing structure is extremely expensive to install as there is no other structure upon which the lift well can use for support, and so it needs to be a free standing structure.

Escalators are often also used to move people from and to the platform. Escalators are very popular because the speed up the departure of people from the platform once passengers have alighted. Escalators can be provided individually, in pairs, or even in groups of three or more.

A Station Escalator

Chapter 6 Customer Support on Stations

Many of the ancillary services provided to passengers during their rail trip are provided at stations. Stations are also the entry point for passengers into the rail system. This is where money changes hands, support services can be provided, and information passed on the passengers about the operation of the rail system.

The trend in recent years has been an increase in the volume of services provided to passengers. Mobile phone reception is now more common un underground stations. Free wifi may be provided. Passenger information is more comprehensive than it was in the past. What services are provided in stations has improved significantly.

Broadly, station design can include many of the services that are provided on stations. The definition of station design can vary, and may not include ancillary services such as communications and wifi. Station design definitely includes the provision of toilets for passengers, and help points and ticketing. This book assumes that station design includes all ancillary services, such as providing clean water, or local maps and tourist information.

Many of the services that can potentially be provided on a station require space for them to be located. The structural design of the station is important, for many reasons, but also to allow the installation of different services to passengers. Small stations may not be able to accommodate the installation of escalators or lifts, as there is no space to put them. Small concourses may limit the number of ticketing machines that can be installed. In general it is best if stations are large to accommodate the installation of additional services should the need arise later in the life of the station.

This chapter will describe some of the more common passenger support systems, and what they can do. They are not mandatory for a station, but customer service is improved where they are provided. Complex engineering systems cost money, and require maintenance and management, and where passenger numbers are low then the justification for installing these systems may not be there.

Some of the customer facilities that can be provided on a station include:

- Toilets
- Covered waiting areas
- Air-conditioning
- Vending machines and food stalls
- Information of all sorts, including tourist information
- Television screens showing news and other information
- First aid
- Internet kiosks
- Wifi
- Free water
- Mobile phone reception
- Prayer rooms
- Breast feeding rooms
- Lockers
- Services with baggage (such as long term storage)
- Sale of rail related souvenirs
- Shops selling all sorts of products
- Banking facilities
- Library facilities for long journeys

In any one station it is unlikely that all of these facilities would be installed simultaneously.

Toilets are not installed in many different systems, although of course they are popular with passengers. The problem with toilets is that they are expensive to maintain, and are focal points for crime. They can also attract the homeless, and drug deals and other crimes can be committed there. Toilets are not always installed, even in the most heavily used systems, and Hong Kong MTR has toilets only in a small number of stations.

Passenger information systems

Passengers need information on when trains are arriving and on which platform. Passenger information systems (PIS) provide this information to passengers, and this can be provided through a variety of different media, such as display boards, telephones, announcements, or through the internet. Recently many railways have set up systems so that apps on smart phones can be installed so that real time information can be obtained for trains and their movements.

Below is a picture of passenger information screens in Central station in Brisbane. This system provides information on when trains are arriving and leaving, and what platform they are on. This system is a good one, and passenger information is clear.

Passenger Information Display

Information other than train running can also be provided to passengers. For example, where train lines are removed for service for major maintenance or upgrading, then information can be provided to passengers on when and where this is happening. Alternatively, when trains are delayed, information should be provided to passengers so that they know where to go to get buses, or what the forecast is for the resumption of services.

The photo below shows an old style timetable display. The older style was able to present a lot of information, and this one has a clock above and the stopping pattern below. In red are the interchange stations. At this station there are two platforms. The name of each station is painted onto a block of wood, which can be turned to display the relevant information for the next train. Whilst this system looks primitive, and it is, in practice it worked quite well. Clearly the station needs to be manned so that staff could come out and change what is displayed after the passage of each train. This type of system has become uncommon, and computerisation has resulted in the removal of many of the timetable displays like the one below.

Wooden Timetable Passenger Display

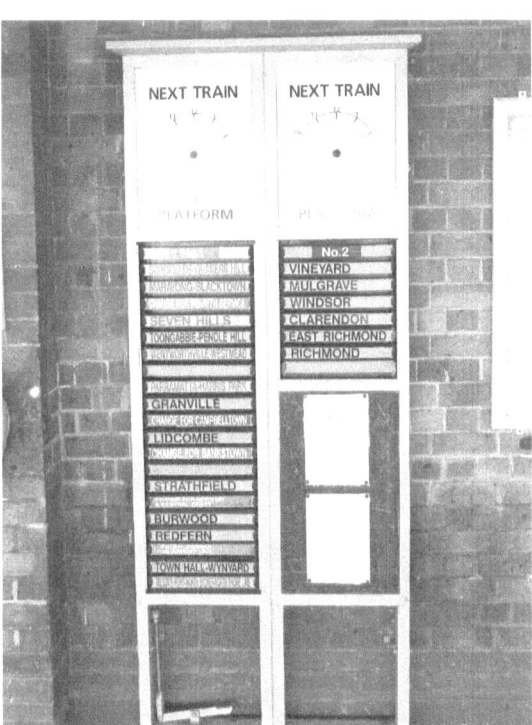

Information on the next available train is also very useful. Often located on station, screens are provided overhead where passengers can look up and see the next train. The picture below shows a simple rail passenger information screen in a metro station in Paris. The information is very basic, but provides what passengers need.

Passenger Information Sign in Paris

Information about the local area can also be provided to passengers. This includes exits, where important landmarks are located, and how to get there from where passengers are standing.

Maps should be provided and easy to read. Network maps in particular should be very common. Below in the two smaller photos are geographical maps provided in two different stations. The one on the left is of the metro network in Tokyo. The one on the right is the regional rail system of Taiwan.

Geographically Correct Maps in Stations

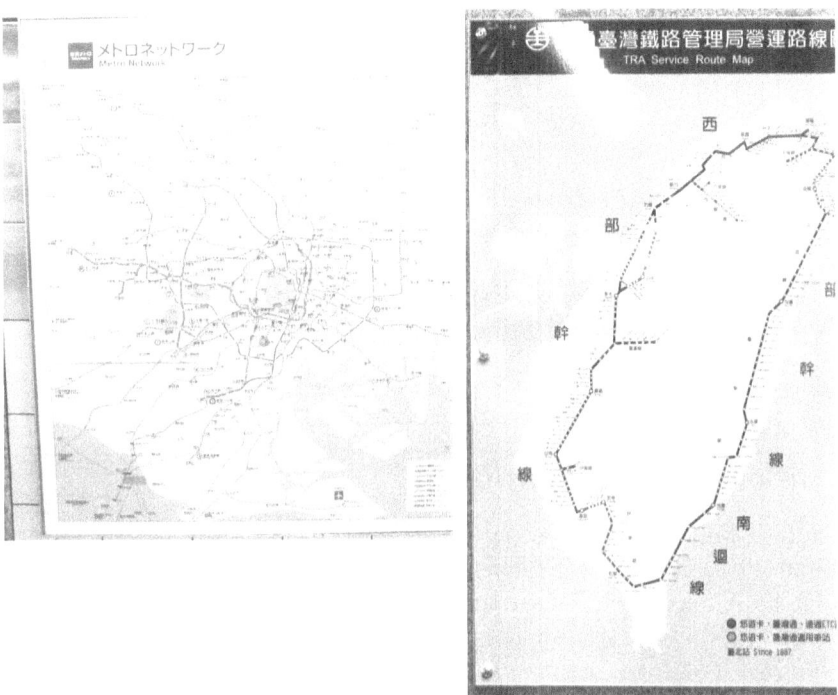

The photo below is of a different type of passenger information. Very long trains, in particular regional and HSR trains, have numbered carriages and can be very long. Their length, and use of reserved seating on HSR trains, means that passengers need to know where their carriage is located. For HSR services where a stop is only a couple of minutes at any one station, passengers need to know where their carriage is located along the platform, and so these signs are provided along the platform to provide this information.

Passenger Carriage Information

Timetable Information

Not all rail systems have passenger timetables, in fact many do not. Metros operate with a frequency that means that timetabling of trains is not really necessary. People arrive at a station and catch the next train, which is only a few minutes away because the frequency of train services is so high. Intermediate capacity rail systems also do not have timetables, for the same reasons as metros, and monorails may or may not have passenger timetables, depending on the frequency of service, but commonly do not have one. Of course the rail operator keeps a working timetable.

For all other train systems timetables are the norm. Timetables provide a time and a stopping pattern for services, and a timetable may either describe the services on the entire rail system, or one part. Timetables when created, and when appropriate, need to be made available to the public. Timetable information can be made available through a variety of different media.

A distinction needs to be made between passenger timetables, and railway working timetables. A railway will usually need to move trains around to get them ready for the next revenue service. Many train trips during the night are made with no passengers, and these services are timetabled, just like trains that carry passengers. Sometimes the timetable that describes all the train trips, including empty trains is called the working timetable. Timetables for complicated systems can be very large and run to hundreds of pages.

Trains in a timetable may or may not be given a train number. Train numbers can be used for ticketing, and when seats can be reserved on a train. A train ticket will need to specify the train number and the seat. There are however, many rail systems where trains are not numbered.

Timetables also need to provide information on the stopping pattern. Trains do not need to stop at every station, and often do not. Express trains will stop at only a small number of stations, and for all other they will pass without stopping. This needs to be clearly indicated in any timetable. Timetabling is discussed in depth in Chapter 23.

Timetables are often available from information counters in railways, as a brochure or a pamphlet. Often it is a small document that easily fits into people's hands. Timetables can also be distributed to customers through small cards that fit into the palm of one's hand, or plastic laminated sheets of paper. Large timetables may take the form of a printed book.

Timetables can also be presented in the form of large boards or posters in stations and at key locations. These boards can be posted up against a wall, or free standing.

Much more commonly now timetables are on websites where passengers can access them. This is a very good way of presenting timetable information to passengers, and web portals with timetable information can be heavily used. Another solution to providing customers with timetable information is to create custom purpose apps, which can be easily searched to find trains arrival and departure times.

Tickets and Ticketing

There are a huge number of different systems, and describing them all would be impossible, but there are some standard systems that are commonly used. The variety of different ways to sell tickets is quite amazing, and there always seems to be another system or method. For many metros ticketing is quite straightforward, with passengers passing through barriers to gain entry and to exit from stations. Many other rail systems also used barriers to control entry and exit into stations.

Grouping ticketing systems into how fares are calculated, we have the following categories:

- Point to point, where the fare is calculated based on the start and end point of the journey. Normally fares are increased as the journey distance increases. Crossing certain places or locations may incur an additional charge, such as a rail tunnel that passes under a body of water.
- Time based, where the ticket allows passengers to travel for a fixed period of time, such as two hours, or even the entire day. Some tickets are issued that apply for entire weeks or even months
- Zonal based tickets, where a ticket entitles the holder to travel within specific zones of the rail system, and only within those zones. Sometimes this is combined with time periods, ie, travel within zone 2 for 2 hours

For long distance travel mostly point to point systems are used to calculate the fare price. There are however, a small number of rail systems where the purchase of a weekly pass provides passengers with the right to travel many times over the network, and this can be for large distances. The high speed rail system in Japan has such a system, and despite the high cost of such passes, many are sold. Each pass entitles the holder to an unreserved seat on certain types of train services in second class for a fixed time.

Passengers on many rail systems need to provide proof of payment to rail staff, or conductors. Passengers may need to retain a paper ticket to show to that payment has been made for the trip that the passenger is making, or where passengers board a train using a smart card, some rail systems have staff that check tickets using a smart card reader. Other rail systems use a barrier system, where passengers gain access to the station by passing through barriers. Ticket prices may be calculated when passengers exit from the station. Any type of ticket fare calculation system can be used, such as a zonal or point to point system which is checked with barriers.

Ticketing on high speed rail and other premium rail services is much more like an aeroplane than a bus or a metro. High speed trains, and other premium train services, trains are numbered and passengers receive seat numbers. In this type of system passengers need to identify which seat they are sitting in, otherwise an argument will arise with other passengers.

Some rail system use an honour system, where passengers are required to pay without any form of compulsion to do so. There is no one to check their tickets or payments, and the rail system simply trusts that the money has been paid. This has been tried in Australia, and the experience was not a happy one, with very few passengers paying anything. In Hong Kong typically a barrier system is used to gain access to stations, but on one line an honour system is used when passengers gain access to first class (that's the train to the border with mainland China). This system seems to work quite well. Overall honour systems for rail ticketing do seem to be rare.

A common system used in Australia for enforcing payment is a little different from the systems mentioned above. In many of the large commuter systems that exist in Australia, there are a small number of city stations, with barriers and staff checking tickets, and large numbers of small suburban stations where very few people get on or off. Typically there might be 5 to 8 inner city stations, and over 150 to 300 other stations. Tickets are checked at the major stations, but not at the small ones. Any passengers that travels from one small station to another essentially travels for free, and everyone else has their ticket checked at the major stations. This system works quite well in most cases.

The old style proof of payment system used printed paper tickets. Old style tickets were often made of paper, with information printed onto them. Before this tickets were often pre-printed, with small writing, and made of fairly hard cardboard. Some of these old tickets were quite pretty to look and, and had a satisfying feel to them. In modern times paper tickets have become rarer, with smart card becoming more common, at least for rail systems that involve short trips within major urban centres. For long distance rail paper tickets are here to stay, at least for the time being.

Below is a picture of some paper tickets from the Perth rail system.

Paper Tickets from Perth Western Australia

Many countries sell tickets where travel on the train is combined with entry to a theme park. The train ticket includes the price of entry. In Sydney tickets are sold that combine the cost of ferry travel, and the train to get to the ferry, with the cost of entry to Sydney Zoo. This type of ticket is frequently created by marketing groups within railways, much to the frustration of stations staff who need to learn all the new tickets and their names.

Smart cards have become much more common in rail systems around the world. A smart card is a card like a credit card where passengers put money and then use the card to enter and exit stations. As passengers pass through station barriers money is deducted from the smart card. There are usually many machines located at stations through which passengers can deposit more money, check transaction history, and see their card balance. Smart cards are extremely common in Asia, less so in Australia. Some common smart cards from Asia and Australia are shown below. The card in the top left is for Kuala Lumpur, and the bottom right is the Octopus card for Hong Kong.

Normally discounts are offered on rail travel for those who have a smart card, as opposed to those who pay with cash.

Smart Cards from Various Railways

Below are some ticket machines in Western Australia. On the right is an add value machine, which is used to add money on to their smart card. In the middle are the machines for selling old style paper tickets.

Ticketing Machines in Perth

Vending Machines and Advertising

Vending machines installed into stations, especially in Asia, are amazing. An extraordinary variety of products are available for sale, including food and drinks, cosmetics, souvenirs, key rings, books, umbrellas, pens, and even clothing. These vending machines are often visually stunning for those who have not seen them before, and some of them contain very unusual items. Whilst not specifically part of the design of a station, adding vending machines that offer a variety of different items can add to the amenity of the station.

The vending machine below is the most remarkable the author has seen. Very large, several metres long, it is located in Taipei main station at the entrance to the HSR platforms. It is a library, and a passenger can buy or borrow books, and the control panel on the right hand side is to select a book. Chinese, Japanese, and some English books were available. The books are intended to be used by passengers on the HSR line, who can read them in the 2.5 hour journey from one end of the system to the other. (The Taiwanese are very educated and read a lot!)

A Lending Library in a Station

Vending machines can be an important source of revenue for railways. Whilst it may not seem important, every source of revenue counts. One vending machine can bring in thousands of dollars (in Australia) per week, and where large numbers of vending machines are installed then the revenue can be considerable.

One major problem with vending machines is vandalism. Vending machines almost always require money to sell goods (although electronic payment seems to be becoming more common), and where there are high levels of violence and property crime then vending machines can be attacked. Whilst in theory it is possible to install CCTV cameras to watch vending machines, in practice protecting them is rather difficult. In many parts of Asia, where this kind of crime is rare, exotic and interesting vending machines are installed in many stations. In some parts of Australia, crime is frequent enough that vending machines cannot be installed due to theft and damage to the machines.

Advertising also can be an important source of revenue for a railway that can be quite cash strapped. Passenger revenue in most railways is rarely sufficient to cover operating costs, and anything that can contribute to the cost of running a railway is welcome. Advertising can bring in substantial revenues, and advertisers will pay for the right to place their advertisements in various parts of the station. MTR in Hong

Kong describes a place where advertising can be placed as an "advertising point".

Stations can be designed to allow for the largest possible number of advertising points. Advertising points are places where passengers will be looking directly at, or walking by. Areas where passengers wait can also be useful for placing advertising. The insides of trains can also be good places to put advertising, and the photo below shows a metro train in Japan with banners reaching down from the ceiling.

Banners in Tokyo Metro

Advertising plays an important part in the revenue earned by Hong Kong MTR. In 2012 Hong Kong MTR earned $130 million US just from advertising. MTR has large numbers of advertising points in station, and many of the tunnels and passages leading to their stations are lined with advertising. It is important to note that the cost of installing and maintaining advertising is not high, and a very high percentage of any revenue earned from advertising can be kept as profit, or contribute towards the cost of running trains.

Advertising is not limited to signage. This display is for digital cameras, in a display cabinet in Thailand. This one is at Chit Lom station in Bangkok, and seems to contain actual digital cameras. Promotions in stations for different products can take a variety of different forms.

An Advertising Display

Many rail companies have taken an aggressive approach to installing advertising and shops within a station. It is possible for railways to earn substantial revenue from a station, and this is particularly true for stations with high numbers of passenger movements. Careful design of a station can return substantial revenue to a rail system, and whilst many stations are not designed to maximise shop and advertising revenue, it is a very effective and powerful way to increase revenue. MTR in Hong Kong is able to generate a substantial profit from running a rail system because of the management of the shop and advertising rights within their stations.

Souvenir Shops

Souvenir shops are sometimes established for railways that are very proud of their construction and operation. These quaint little shops are located near the centre of the rail system, and are often quite small and may be overlooked by the casual passer by. There are a number of these in South East Asia.

The photo below is of the souvenir shop in Hong Kong. It sells models of trains that operate on its network, as well as cup holders, pens, T shirts, stationary with MTR branding, and mouse pads. The souvenir shop also doubles as a ticket sales office.

A Rail Souvenir Shop

There is no harm in installing a souvenir shop for a railway. It promotes pride in the rail system, and generates free marketing. It's probably a good idea for a souvenir shop to be included in the design of a really good quality railway. It provides an opportunity for the citizens of the area where the railway operates to demonstrate their appreciation of the railway, and support it by using its merchandising. It also reflects well on the railway that people would want to buy its products, and can be an effective way of demonstrating that the railway is operated efficiently and in a way that suits its customers.

Other Infrastructure

Bins are often provided on stations, but with the increase in terrorism, many of the bins were removed from stations in Australia. The fear was that terrorists would place a bomb in the bin, then leave, allowing the bomb to go off and them to escape. A solution was found to this problem by having transparent bins. In theory any bomb would be seen before it would explode. The picture below shows this type of bin. The photo was taken at Tokyo high speed station.

Transparent Rubbish Bins in Tokyo

REFERENCES

1. Infrabel, *Network Statement*, Version of 9/12/2011

2. banedanmark, *Network Statement,* 2012, Jan 2011

3. Liang, H. & Ning, Z. & Yana, S *Analysis and Selection on Fare System of Urban Rail Transit*, Advanced Management Science (ICAMs), 2010

Chapter 7 Geometry, Heights and Grades and Platform Gaps

The geometry and design of the track of a rail system has a dramatic impact upon the design of stations. Track design can strongly influence how a station is structured and designed, and rail systems with high track curves and superelevation will have wider and larger platform gaps. This chapter discusses how track design impacts on stations, especially for platform gaps.

Platform gaps are a common thing in many rail systems. Platform gaps, if too large, cause difficulties for passengers to board and alight from trains. Minimising a platform gap is a important part of the design of any new railway station.

Curves and superelevation, even a small amount, at a station will result in large platform gaps. It is best for minimising the gap if there is no superelevation, and no curve in track. Below are presented calculations that demonstrate just how large the gap can become. The author has seen platform gaps in excess of 30 cm (1 foot), and in some cases even bigger. This size of gap is considered very undesirable for any new station.

Superelevation is a difference in level in the two rails, with one being higher than another. Again, at a station, it is best if there is no superelevation at all, and passengers step into a level train. Where the superelevation is steep, this tilts the train, resulting in a floor which is at an angle to the ground, and potentially there is a risk that passengers will stumble and fall when boarding and alighting. Small amounts of superelevation are tolerable at stations, large amounts are not, and what reasonable limits are for the design of any new station is quite low.

Loading and structure gauge is a term that applies to the space through which a train moves. Structure gauge is the space that the infrastructure must stay out of for a train to make its way through a rail system. This includes platforms, where platform edges must not intrude into the structure gauge to the point where a train will strike the platform when entering a station. Platform strikes are uncommon, and when they occur can cause serious damage to a train. Usually the paint is stripped from the side of the train next to the platform.

The size of platform gaps is a function of both the superelevation and the curvature of track. Both are undesirable, and what is best is straight flat track which provides a better closer fit of the train to the station. Where there is curvature and superelevation, the loading gauge increases, and so does the structure gauge. This includes platforms at stations.

Loading and Structure Gauge

Railways have specific terms for describing the space required for a train to pass through on a network. These terms are commonly used, and understood between countries. These terms are a rare example of some jargon that is used in Australia/UK and the US interchangeably. They are:
- Structure gauge
- Loading gauge
- Kinematic envelope

The structure gauge is a defined space around the track, into which no equipment or infrastructure is permitted. If any equipment strays into that space, then a train may strike it as is comes past. The structure gauge is the space allocated to trains to pass along the track and is larger than the train that passes through it, to allow for movement of the train and any possible slight deviations of the train from its design size. Trains are never as large as the structure gauge.

Structure gauge is what infrastructure maintainers use for any maintenance. Maintainers need clear cut guidance on what the structure gauge is, and any large railway and many smaller ones will have detailed standards on structure gauge and what sizes are required. It is not sufficient for an infrastructure maintainer to be told the loading gauge, as this is information is not useful and cannot be used for maintenance purposes.

The loading gauge is the area in which a train must fit in when stationary. Loading gauge is relevant to rollingstock and its design. It's important because the loading gauge determines which trains can be bought, what size they are, and hence their capacity. Loading gauges are quite important, and some of the more common loading gauges are listed below.

The kinematic envelope is the space through which a train might move, taking into account superelevation (cant), the suspension of the train, the end throw and centre throw. Calculating the kinematic envelope is a process called dynamic gauging. Calculating the kinematic envelope can be a paper exercise, and there are formulas that describe how to do this. The kinematic envelope increases where there are curves, as the curves result in the end of the train protruding away from the track.

Whilst changes to structure gauge are a common type of rail transport project, the cost can be high. Changes to structure gauge are very expensive, and can involve large scale changes to infrastructure. To complete a change from one structure gauge to a larger one, every point in a rail system or rail line needs to be converted, it's not sufficient to convert some or even most of the track. There is no benefit for doing most of it, and so one problematic point in a rail system can stop the conversion to a larger structure gauge. This needs to be considered in any rail transport planning.

In many cases the maximum possible loading and structure and loading gauge is fixed. Train lines often pass next to structures and buildings that cannot be moved or demolished, and so it is not possible to change the width of the train, or the space through which the train passes. Some stations are heritage listed, and so major changes are not possible. In these cases rail operators need to manage their rollingstock as best they can, given the constraints on size. Problems with the maximum permitted size of trains can be very expensive to manage.

Loading gauges are often not square or rectangular. The diagram below shows a typical profile of a loading gauge. The shape down below is typical of what a loading gauge outline looks like. Whilst not always this shape, they often are, and so a train that is a perfect rectangle would not be permitted to operate on many rail networks if it were above a certain size.

Figure 7.1 Typical Loading Gauge

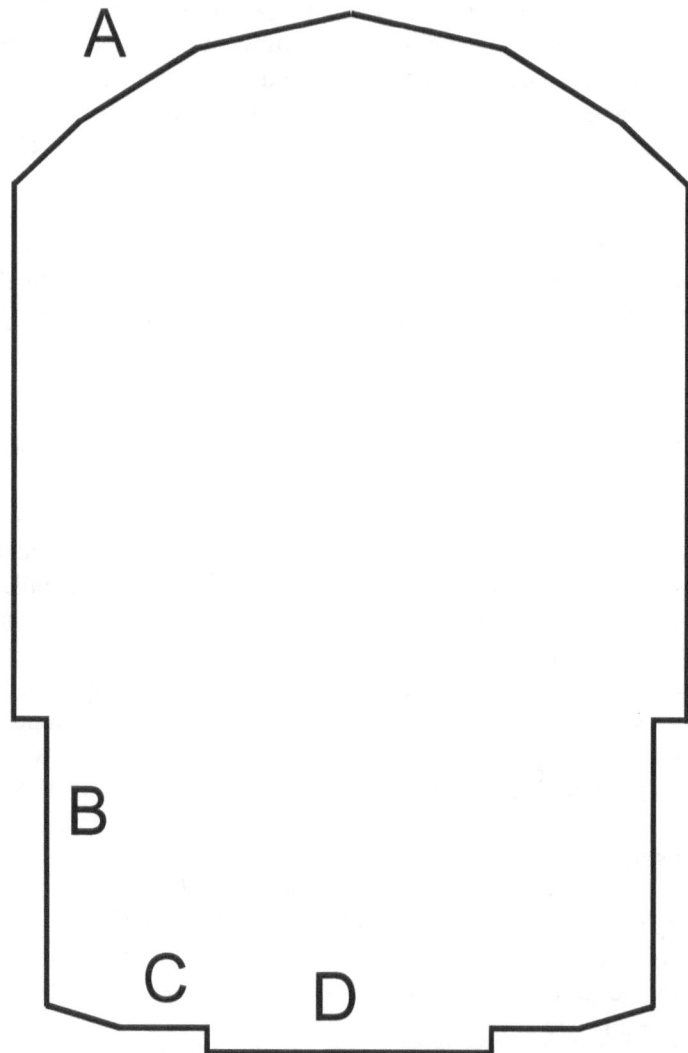

The letters in the diagram above refer to various parts of the outline. These are:

A/ This is the curved part of the roof of the train. Most passenger loading gauges are curved, and this allows the construction of arch shaped tunnels, which are cheaper to construct than tunnels with rectangular rooves in many cases.

B/ There are often cut-outs for platforms for passenger trains. There is always a risk that passengers will fall between the train and the platform, and it's best if this gap is kept as small as possible. One way of managing this is to have the train overhang the platform, so that the gap is minimised.

C/ For the bottom of the train the loading gauge is flat and even all the way along, and is higher is some parts compared to others. In the schematic above at the sides of the loading gauge, the loading gauge does not extend down to the bottom of the train (same as D). This is to allow the many different types of rail side devices to operate and exist. Also the ballast is sometimes too high, and so contact with the ballast is minimised by having the train higher than the track.

D/ This is the lowest part of the train, and where the train runs along the track.

In the worst possible case the kinematic envelope should still be within the structure gauge. If the kinematic envelope extends to the structure gauge or beyond it, then trains may strike objects and structures next to the track (such as platforms). The kinematic envelope needs to fall within the structure gauge.

Obviously one way to determine the kinematic envelope is to run different trains along the track and see what happens. Whilst this is possible, it is far better to calculate the kinematic envelope, because if a train strikes an object it tends to make a bit of a mess, and the damage can be substantial. Also once a rail line is constructed it can be a bit difficult for the structure gauge to be changed, so any errors can have a very long term impact. So for almost all rail projects in the anywhere, the kinematic envelope will be calculated first before construction begins.

So of the things that need to be considered in the calculation of a kinematic envelope are:
- The superelevation of the track
- Track movement
- The suspension of the train
- Loads on the train, for example, fully loaded passenger trains compared to empty ones
- Rail wear
- Tilting functions of trains, including both passive and active tilt

- Curves in the track

Structure, loading gauge and the kinematic envelope are most relevant to a railway in tunnels, but are also important at stations and particularly at platforms. Tunnels have very limited space available, and increasing the size of the tunnel once constructed is a messy and expensive business. If a train can't fit into a tunnel, there is little a rail organisation can do to get it to fit in, other than making major engineering changes. Some things can be done, and trains with hard suspensions and very little movement in the springs that support the train can move through slightly smaller tunnels. Also, trains that move at lower speeds can also fit into smaller tunnels, as they bounce around less when moving at lower speeds. Where a railway needs to move a large train through a small structure gauge, this can sometimes be achieved with dramatically reducing the speeds of the train to a point where the railway is confident that the train will not strike any object.

If a train strikes an object such as a platform the result can be very bad indeed. Whilst a glancing blow may not be very serious, a full impact with a fixed object is really a train crash, and passengers can be killed. That's really bad, so railways will put a lot of effort into ensuring that trains cannot collide with anything fixed. One of the key responsibilities of maintenance staff is to ensure that a collision does not occur.

Vegetation often will grow into the space where the train runs. Trees often line rail corridors, and as trees grow they can come into contact with passing trains. This can be very common in some networks, and it's common in Australia. It's mostly harmless for trains to brush alongside trees, and most tree branches are quite soft. Trees can present problems to the overhead wiring system, or reduce the visibility of signals so that drivers cannot see them. In these situations trees can be a problem, or when they fall over in a big storm this can also block running lines.

In some cases trees may be planted on stations. The branches of trees may grow to the point where they intrude into the structure gauge, and even strike a train. Trees on stations, where they are healthy and continue to grow, will need to be routinely pruned to keep them outside of the structure gauge

It has become common to calculate the movement of trains, and the swept volume resulting from this, with software. Some software packages have been written which work quite well. The software can visually display and calculate the movement of trains through tunnels, and so any problem areas that need to be addressed are identified. Whilst a hand calculation is possible, this method is increasingly rarely used. The calculation of the structure and loading gauges and a key part of the planning process, but given the technical detail necessary, and the cost, and the level of detail needed to carry out the analysis, this would typically be done very late in the process (but definitely before construction).

Loading gauges, as mentioned above, often have complicated shapes. To simplify things, they are often described in terms of height and width. This is shown below.

Figure 7.2 Simplified Description of Train Size

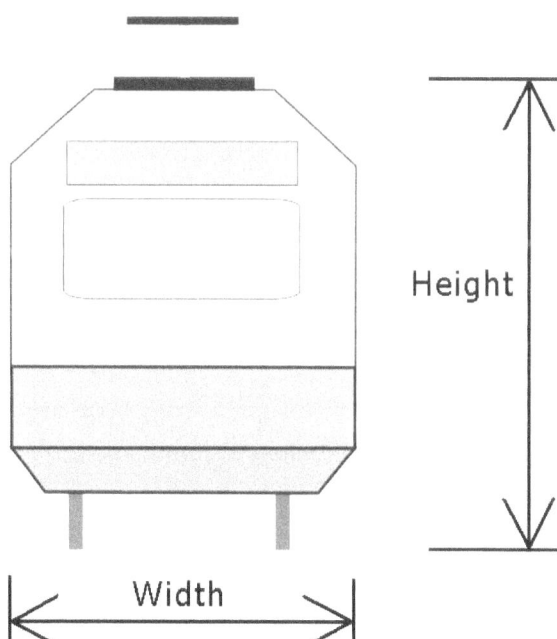

The pantograph above the train is not usually included in the loading gauge. In practice the pantograph is spring loaded so it can move up and down, and can usually be pushed down almost flat with the top of the train. Where the pantograph sits there is usually a hole/recess so that it can be strapped down, i.e. when transporting the train by sea. The space where the pantograph is compressed into is called the pantograph well.

Below are some common loading gauges. It is only a small selection of the large number of loading gauges currently in use. Worldwide there would be hundreds of different loading gauges, and probably no person would be familiar with them all.

\multicolumn{3}{c}{Table of Loading Gauges}		
Country	Name	Width	Height
UK	W6	2820 (9 feet 4 inches)	3965 (13 feet)
	W7	2778 (9 feet 1 inch)	3966 (13 feet)
	W9	2996 (9 feet 10 inches)	3967 (13 feet)
	C1	2744 (9 feet)	3772 (12 feet 4.5 inches)
(high speed)	UK1	2720 (8 feet 11 inches)	3965 (13 feet)
US, Canada, Mexico	AAR plate B	3250 (10 feet 8 inches)	4620 (15 feet 2 inches)
	AAR plate C	3251 (10 feet 8 inches)	4720 (15 feet 6 inches)
	AAR plate E	3252 (10 feet 8 inches)	4800 (15 feet 9 inches)
	AAR plate F	3253 (10 feet 8 inches)	5180 (17 feet)
European Union	UIC-A	3150 (10 feet 4 inches)	4320 (14 feet 2 inches)
	UIC-B	3151 (10 feet 4 inches)	4321 (14 feet 2 inches)
	UIC-C	3152 (10 feet 4 inches)	4650 (15 feet 3 inches)
Germany	G1	3153 (10 feet 4 inches)	4280 (14 feet 0.5 inches)

	G2	3154 (10 feet 4 inches)	4650 (15 feet 3 inches)
Spain/Portugal	Iberian gauge	3300 (10 feet 10 inches)	4300 (14 feet 1 inch)

Centre and End Throw

Below are some of the formulas used to calculate the kinematic envelope. Formulas for centre and end throw are shown, as well as the effect of superelevation. Train carriages are not flexible (but some are articulated), and so around curves more room is needed (including for articulated trains). End throw is the distance the centre of the end of the train protrudes away from the centre of the track. Centre throw is the distance between the centre of the train and the centre of the track. Only over curved track are the centres of the train and track in different places (looking down onto the train of course).

Trains sweep through a larger volume when passing through a curve. The end and centre of the carriage is no longer over the centre of the track, and this makes the volume occupied by the train larger. Most train carriages are fixed and rigid, and don't bend and are not articulated. Trains with a large number of articulated sections can bend in many places, and light rail vehicles often have many of these. This will reduce the size of the structure gauge needed. Longer and faster trains such as regional or commuter trains will have only a small number of couplings between carriages and sets, and these are the only places where these trains can bend to move around curves. Longer carriages require larger structure gauges compared to the loading gauge.

It should be remembered that trains are a long rectangular box supported by two pivot points each sitting above a bogie. The bogie is the set of wheels on which the carriage is supported. The bogie contains wheels which sit on top of the rails and support the carriage. The geometry of this is shown below:

Figure 7.3 Centre Throw

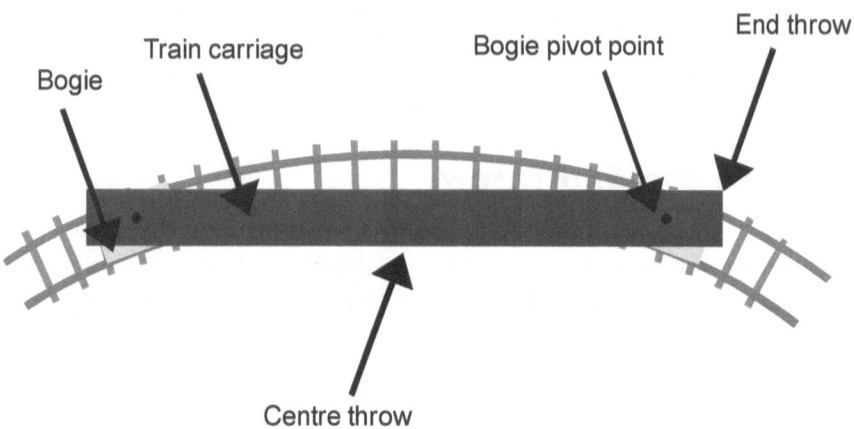

The purple shows a single carriage, and the ends of the carriage jut out beyond the track. Track would not normally (except for light rail and trams) be highly curved, and the curvature is exaggerated to show what is happening. Notice that in the middle of the track the carriage is not above the track, and actually sits over the edge of the track. It is because of all this that the space swept out by a train, as it moves along the track, is larger than the physical size of the carriage. The kinematic envelope is larger than the size of the train, especially for curves.

The extent to which the train stretches away from the track at the ends of the carriage is called the end throw. The greater the curvature of the track, the higher the end throw. The same is true for the centre of the carriage, but on the other side of the track.

One way to achieve efficiencies in train operations is to run the longest possible train carriages whilst keeping the total length of the train constant. Trains with long carriages will be cheaper to procure, as the cost of a carriage increases only slowly with increasing the length of a carriage if at all. Increasing the length of carriages results in the end and centre throw being larger, and so the required structure gauge then increases.

One of the most commonly used formulas for centre throw is:

$$\text{Centre throw} = C_t = \frac{B_c^2}{8R}$$

Where:

C_t = centre throw in metres
R = radius of the curve in metres
B_c = distance between bogie centres in metres

The formula for the centre throw, and how it is obtained, is shown below:

Figure 7.4 Centre Throw Geometry

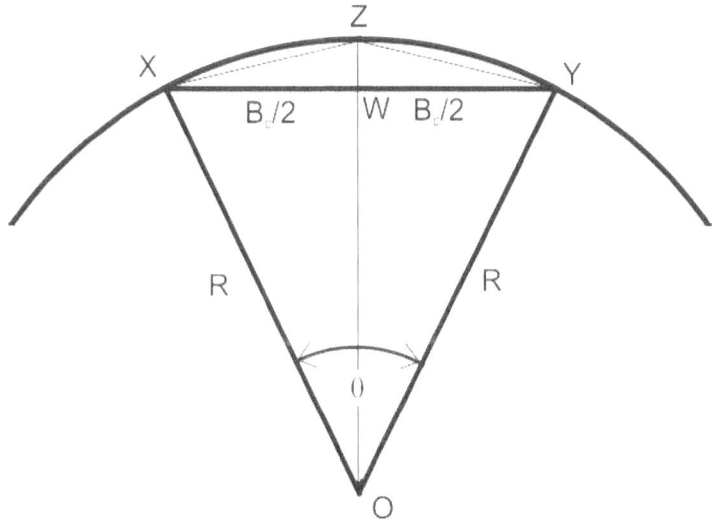

The curve is the track, and the radius R is the track radius. O is the centre of the arc. Points X and Y represent the centre of the bogies. The centre throw is represented by the distance between Z and W, which the distance the centre of the train is moved from the centre of the track because of the curvature of the track. The distance B_c is the distance between the centre of the two bogies.

So, to derive the equation, we have the following:

$$\angle XOZ = 2\angle ZYX$$

And as an approximation we can say:

$$ZY \approx \frac{R\theta}{2}$$

As we have used the formula:

$$\text{Arc length} = \text{Radius} \times \text{subtended angle}$$

And we note that:

$$\angle XYZ = \frac{\theta}{4}$$

As the angle subtended by points at the centre is half that at the circumference.

So using the sine rule we get:

$$\sin\left(\frac{\theta}{2}\right) = \frac{B_c}{2R} \approx \frac{\theta}{2}$$

And we simplify this to get:

$$\theta = \frac{B_c}{R}$$

Examining the triangle ZWY we note that:

$$\tan\left(\frac{\theta}{4}\right) = \frac{C_t}{B_c/2}$$

And noting that $B_c = R\theta$ and substituting:

$$\tan\left(\frac{\theta}{4}\right) = \frac{C_t}{R\theta/2}$$

Using the small angle approximation, we note that:

$$\tan\left(\frac{\theta}{4}\right) \approx \frac{\theta}{4}$$

And we re-arrange this to get:

$$C_t = \frac{R\theta^2}{8}$$

And finally substituting back into the equation we obtain:

$$Centre\ throw = C_t = \frac{B_c^2}{8R}$$

Whilst the equation uses an approximation, it is still very accurate because the length of the carriage is very small compared to the track radius.

The graph below provides a worked example for the size of centre throw for bogie centres of 20 metres and a track radius of 200 metres or more. 200 metres is actually a very tight curve, and most railways would not permit track radii this tight in new construction unless there were very special circumstances requiring it.

Centre Throw (metres) for Bogies centre = 20 metres

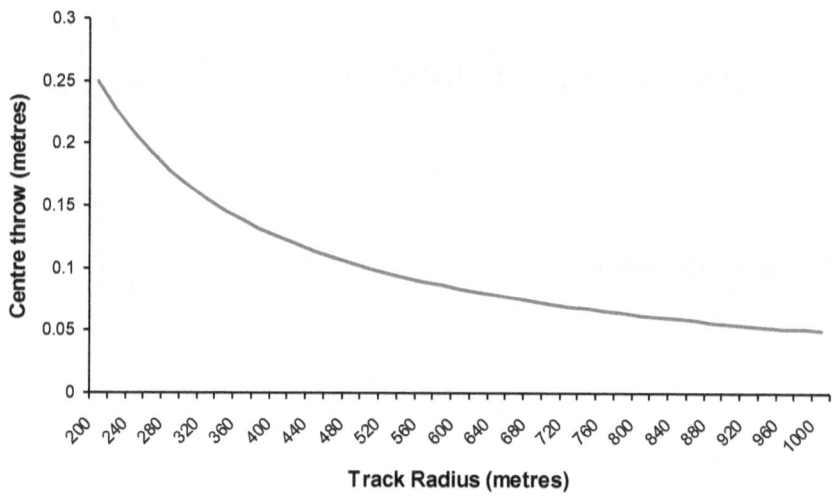

Note that 25 cm is a little less than a foot in the imperial system of measurements. Whilst this might not seem much, it can present major problems in many ways. Tunnels will need to be larger, and the structure gauge will need to be widened. Whilst the additional width required for the rail corridor might not seem much, many railways are terribly constrained with the amount of space they have and may not be able to widen the structure gauge this much.

Also consider that where there is large curvature in the track at a platform, a gap will appear between the carriage and the platform, especially where the carriage door is in the middle of the carriage. 25 cm is often too large for a gap between the carriage and the platform, and where a railway is not prepared to accept such a large gap then the station should not be constructed where the curvature is so large.

One consequence of this formula is that rollingstock that has a shorter distance between bogie centres can be wider, or a carriage with longer bogie centres needs to be narrower. The graph below shows the general principle, for the case where the nominal width of the train is 3 metres with a minimum track radius of 200 metres. As the train gets longer, then the minimum width for a train required to fit into the same structure gauge shrinks.

Maximum train width R = 200 metres

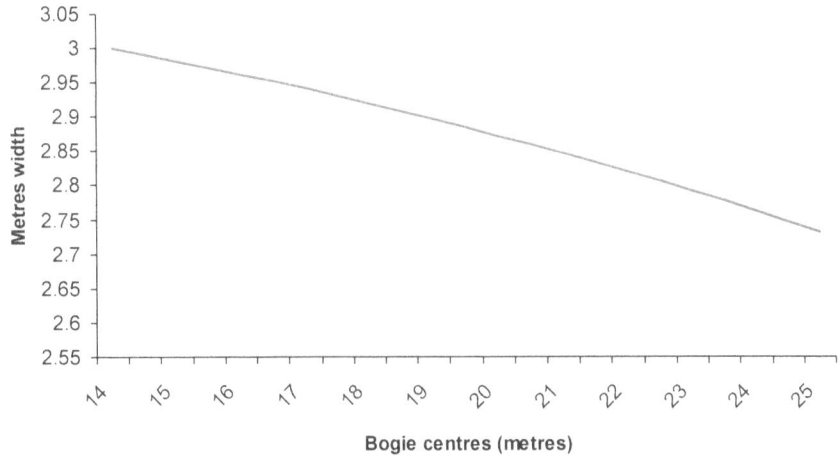

The schematic below shows the calculation and the geometry required for the formula for end throw. End throw is where the end of the carriage sticks out from the track, and overhangs the cess.

On the diagram above we see that the track is represented by GXZYH. This curve approximates what the track could look like with aggressive curvature. The train itself is represented by AF, and the bogie pivot points are located at X and Y. The end throw is represented by AG, which is the tangent to the track from the end of the carriage to the closest point on the curved track.

Figure 7.5 End Throw Geometry

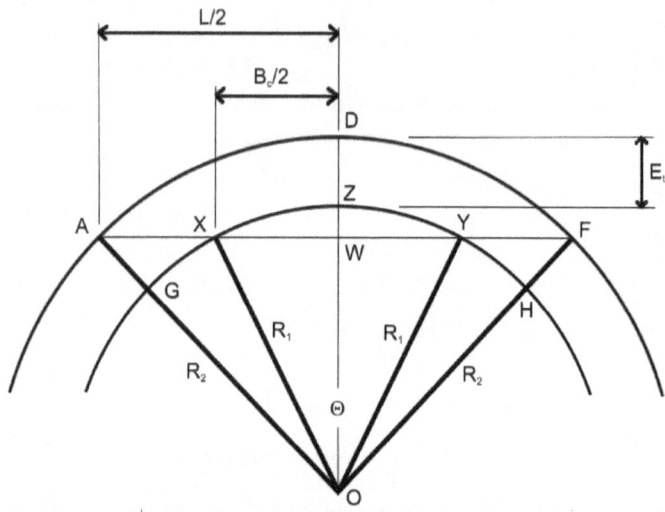

On the diagram above the centre throw is the distance ZW. The formula for centre throw is:

$$Centre\ throw = \frac{B_c^2}{8R_1}$$

Likewise the distance DW can be found from this equation:

$$DW = \frac{L^2}{8R_2}$$

We note of course that DZ = AG = end throw, so the formula for end throw is:

$$End\ throw = DZ = DW - ZW = \frac{L^2}{8R_2} - \frac{B_c^2}{8R_1}$$

If we make the assumption that $R_1 \approx R_2$, which is a fairly good approximation, then we have this equation:

$$\text{End throw} \approx \frac{L^2 - B_c^2}{8R}$$

So what does all this mean? Well, centre and end throw need to be added to the platform gap, otherwise the train will strike the platform at one end. A very short radius curve on track throughout a platform will result in a very large platform gap, especially where rail carriages are very long. Remember, for those with disabilities, large platform gaps are a real problem, and should be eliminated where possible.

Superelevation (Cant)

In determining the kinematic envelope, an allowance must be made for superelevation. Remember that superelevation is the difference in height between the rails. Superelevations of zero are common, especially in freight networks. However, where the superelevation is not zero, this needs to be considered in any calculation for the kinematic envelope.

Figure 7.6 Tunnels with Superelevation

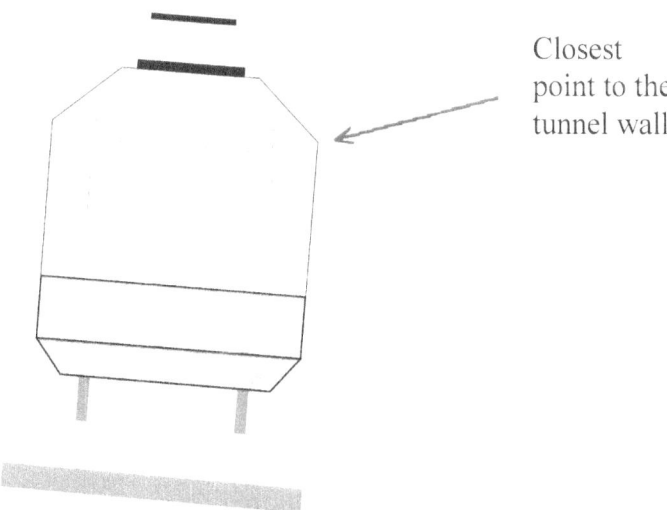

Closest point to the tunnel wall

The schematic above shows that happens in a tunnel when a train moves over a track with superelevation. Note that one of the rails is higher than another, and so the train is tilted over to one side. As tunnels walls are usually or often vertical, the train gets closer to the wall. It is also clear that the relevant point to calculate is the highest point where the train is widest. The calculation for how much the train moves closer to the wall is very simple, and using similar triangles:

$$Z = movement\ towards\ wall = \frac{super}{gauge} \times height$$

Some typical values would be a gauge of 1435mm and a superelevation of 100 millimetres, and a height of about 3 metres. The train in this example would be about 200 millimetres closer to the wall than compared to train running on tracks with no superelevation.

Note that the height would normally be calculated from the top of the rail to the highest widest point on the rollingstock.

Calculating Platform Gaps

The calculation of the size of a platform gap is a difficult calculation because it involves several factors that cannot be expressly calculated. A number of factors need to be considered, and this requires detailed information on the performance of different types of infrastructure and rollingstock.

The platform gap is calculated in two directions; vertically and horizontally. The vertical gap is somewhat easier to control; the horizontal gap can be very large. The combination of the two gives a measure of the acceptability of a gap.

The different factors that need to be considered include:
- Track infrastructure
- Rollingstock
- Centre and end throw
- Superelevation

We note that platforms need to be designed to accept the largest train. Where rollingstock is differently sized, then the platform gap will be larger for smaller and narrower trains. Where one type of rollingstock has a much larger loading gauge than any others, platform gaps may become very large indeed.

The platform gap for any station can be calculated in terms of an expected average gap, and a lower and upper bound in the size of the gap. The lower bound, the minimum, should be greater than 0, otherwise a train may strike the platform. The upper bound is the size of the gap that results if all conditions are at their worst. The upper bound for platform gaps is the one used for infrastructure planning.

To calculate the average gap, the lower and upper bound, consideration is given of the four factors listed above. The superelevation and centre and end throw can be calculated explicitly, and the other two factors need to have some numbers attached to them. For each of these factors, a lower and upper bound can be calculated, or estimated from an operational railway, and then used to estimate the size of the platform gap.

One of the main considerations in setting a minimum distance for the structure gauge is movement of the track. It might seem strange that the track can move, but it sometimes happens, especially on curves. The track structure can move within the ballast, and this is common, especially after maintenance activities (and particularly tamping). Where the track is not particularly stable, or where the ballast has been disturbed, then track movements can be very large, even metres. In this case it is the responsibility of the civil maintenance crew to remedy this problem, which is done with varying degrees of efficiency.

Most rollingstock manufacturers will have a good idea on how their rollingstock moves about as it moves along the track. That's a good place to start, but the operating local railway will know about local conditions and materials. The suspension of the rollingstock is particularly important, and this is what controls the extent of any rolling for a train.

For example, in Sydney the rollingstock is mostly about 3.1 metres wide, and so can be expected to be about 1.6 metres from the centre of the track to the side of the rollingstock. The value normally used for the minimum possible structure gauge is about 2.05 metres from track centres, so about 45 centimetres more than the size of the largest train. This number has been determined through years of experience, and observation of the movement of track in the local area and managed using the maintenance practices in use in that area.

One solution to the need to reduce the platform gap is to use concrete slab track, which moves very little. There are many advantages and disadvantages of this track system, and one key advantage is that the track moves relatively little. This is particularly suitable for tunnels, as the tunnel can be smaller as the minimum structure gauge can be a little smaller.

People with disabilities wish to use trains and public transport want to gap to be as small as possible. The smaller, the better, and with a small platform gap those with disabilities will be able to alight and board without assistance. Where the gap is too wide, a ramp will need top be provided for those with mobility problems, such as those in wheelchairs, or mothers with prams.

An acceptable platform gap, for the horizontal is around 50 to 75 mm, and about 15 to 20 mm in the vertical. Larger than this, the gap starts to present problems for those with disabilities. For very strong people, they can surmount the gap, but the larger the gap, the more difficult this will be.

Platform Heights

Normally all the platforms on a network would be the same height. This is the ideal, and new modern networks are constructed such that all the platforms are the same height. However, in many older rail systems, there is more than one platform height, and potentially there could be several different standard heights. This situation presents tremendous headaches for rail planners, especially when ordering new rollingstock.

Platforms are often not at the same height as the train floor. It is a preference for modern train systems to have the platform as close as possible to the floor of the train, and at the same height, but this often does not happen. The photo below shows the regional tilt train in Taiwan, and note that the floor of the train is higher than the platform, and there is a step between the train and the platform.

Taiwanese Train with Door Flaps

The step fills the space between the train and the platform. The step is often slightly higher than the platform, so that if the platform is curved or too close to the train then the step won't hit the platform.

Platform heights have been decreasing over time. This is especially true for trams and light rail, where platform heights are dropping significantly. Trams often run at street level, and stepping into a high floor tram can be quite daunting, especially for people with disabilities. It's best for disabled people getting into trams to have the floor as low as possible. It is seen as desirable to reduce the height of platforms as much as possible, and rollingstock manufacturers are often keen to announce any reductions in floor heights of their products.

It is engineering challenging to make the floor of the tram very low. Ultra-low floor trams have had some significant engineering problems, with cracks developing in the body of the trams, which were quite serious and needed substantial repairs. The lower floor puts higher forces on the body of the tram, and these stresses can cause higher maintenance costs and maintenance problems.

Ultra-low floor trams, despite their engineering problems, are very helpful to customers. The step up into the tram is a small one, often only 180mm, which is very small. This is enough for people to comfortably enter the tram from road level, and so this technology is still being developed (and perfected).

Low floor trams are higher than ultra-floor trams, and are about 300-350mm from the ground or platform, or about 1 foot in the English imperial system of measurement. Most people can negotiate this kind of step up from the road.

Higher speed trains will generally require higher platforms, at least as high as 550mm. The higher platform allows for structural changes in the rollingstock that make it stronger, and allow for higher speeds. Trams and light rail vehicles with ultra-low floors are limited in speed to about 100 kms/hr, or perhaps even lower.

Where the platform is a different height to the floor of the train, the preference is to make the floor of the train higher. Passengers will step up into the train, and not down. It is considered by some that it's dangerous for passengers to step down into a train, and so this configuration is avoided if at all possible.

There are many different platform heights in use around the world today. The variety is enormous, although attempts are being made to standardise to specific heights. It seems that 550mm is the minimum height for larger commuter trains, although 760 mm platforms are also used. In Australia and Hong Kong platform heights of 1100mm are used, which is high enough that if passengers fall off the platform onto the tracks then they will injured from the fall.

Rarely rollingstock is designed that can accommodate different platform heights. This can be achieved through steps that can vary in height to allow for the different platform heights. Rollingstock with this feature can be very expensive.

European Union decision 2002/735/EC specifies that high speed trains should be designed to a platform height of 550mm or 760mm. However, for trains that operate in the UK 915mm was specified, and for the Netherlands 840mm was specified. Even within a standard designed to force uniformity between member states, there is significant differences in the platform heights.

Where platform height are different throughout a network and there is a need to extend the system, a rail planner faces a number of choices:
1/ modify the existing platforms to a standard height
2/ have two different sets of platform heights, and different rollingstock that is designed for each
3/ continue with different platform heights, and order specialised rollingstock that can accommodate different platform heights.
4/ Design very long platforms that have two different heights, and so able to accept different trains with different floor heights

It's always best to have one standard height throughout a rail system, but there are many examples where this was not possible.

Grades

Track grades should not be installed in stations where possible. In some cases it may be necessary to install a grade at a station, but this is very undesirable, and should only be done where absolutely necessary.

Grades are calculated as below:

Figure 7.7 Grades

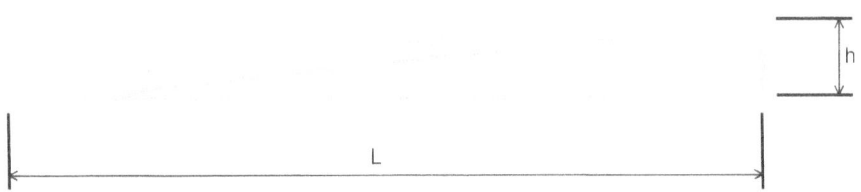

Grades, or sometimes called slopes, can be expressed as percentages, based on this simple formula:

$$Grade = \frac{height}{length} \times 100\%$$

In Australia and the UK grades can be expressed as 1 in X, where X can be found from the formula below:

$$\frac{1}{X} = \frac{height}{length}$$

Which can be re-arranged to give:

$$X = \frac{length}{height}$$

Another way of expressing grades is using this symbol (‰). This symbol is similar to a percentage, but actually means the parts out of 1000. So a 1% grade would be expressed as 10‰. This symbol is common in continental Europe, for the maximum possible grades that a particular type of train can climb. On Wikipedia the symbol is referred to a *"per mille"*, which is Latin for per one thousand.

So, the conversion tables for the grades are:

Grades and Conversions			
%	UK/Australia	Degrees	‰
1	1 in 100	0.57°	10
2	1 in 50	1.15°	20
3	1 in 33	1.72°	30
4	1 in 25	2.29°	40
5	1 in 20	2.86°	50
6	1 in 16.6	3.43°	60
7	1 in 14.3	4.00°	70
8	1 in 12.5	4.57°	80
9	1 in 11.1	5.14°	90
10	1 in 10	5.71°	100
11	1 in 9.1	6.28°	110
12	1 in 8.3	6.84°	120
13	1 in 7.7	7.41°	130

Most rollingstock is quite limited in the grade that it can climb. Common limits for the grades that rollingstock can climb are listed below, with some comments:

Maximum Acceptable Grades		
Rollingstock type	Max grade	Comments
Trams	6% or 10% with specially designed rollingstock	Some trams are specially designed to climb high grades
Light rail	6% or 10% with specially designed rollingstock	As more vehicles are combined into a consist, the total possible grade may be reduced
Commuter rail	3%	These trains are not designed to climb high grades
Regional rail	3%	
Freight	1.5%	Typically higher grades make the freight service uneconomical, as more locomotives are needed
High speed rail	1.5%	Higher grades tend to have a large speed penalty
Monorails	6%	Able to climb fairly steep grades
Metros	3%	Steel on steel metros
Metros (rubber tyred)	12%	Very large grades can be accepted

A typical limit for a grade at a station is 1 in 100. Whilst larger grades can be accepted, it is generally preferable to limit grades at stations as much as possible.

Where a rail system has high grades, and there are frequent station, problems arise. The grades may be needed to get the trains to the right height at each station. However high grades at stations are undesirable, and present safety risks for customers. If a 1 in 100 grade is acceptable for stations, and 5 in 100 are needed, what happens at the stations?

There are a number of solutions to this problem, and some of these are:

1/ stations are built with a low grade, and the grade elsewhere is increased to compensate
2/ stations may need to be either higher or lower, which may mean a really deep station to accommodate the flat grade through the station
3/ the spacing between stations may need to be increased, to allow for trains to climb to the correct height for a flat station
4/ in the worse case, stations may not be installed at all, and the entire station removed from any design. This will eliminate the problem obviously, but can be a very problematic solution.

Chapter 8 Nearby Centres and Facilities

An important part of the design of a station is the nearby facilities. The function and purpose of a station is almost always improved by the additional of useful facilities in and around a station. The presence of these facilities increases passenger numbers, makes the use of the station more attractive, and can have many secondary benefits such as improving passenger security around the station.

Facilities such as shopping centres and apartment buildings are valuable, and constructing them can bring substantial profits to the developer. This profit can contribute to the cost of a construction of a rail system, and the rents to the operational cost, and so adding facilities can greatly assit with the construction of any rail system. This makes this topic important, and so for station design, gets its own chapter.

Adding shopping centres and other facilities to stations can substantially improve the number of people moving through the station. Large facilities, such as shopping centres, can increase the number of people using the rail system dramatically, and can turn a quiet thinly used station into a very busy one. Placing large facilities next to rail stations is a very good strategy when planning rail systems, so much so that it has a name; Transport Orientated Development (TOD).

Overall it adds greatly to the convenience and liveability of a city by allowing passengers to get to major facilities by rail. Tourists often find the rail system very convenient to use when visiting a major city for the first time, because the maps for rail systems are often well laid out and easy to understand, and unlike bus systems rail systems are permanent and rarely change. Connecting airports especially to a rail system can greatly assist tourists within a city, and tourism can bring in a lot of revenue to a country.

As a policy decision it may be decided to connect major facilities to the rail system, and very large venues are usually connected to the rail system. Venues where the Olympic Games are held are always connected to the rail system, and a rail line may be constructed just for this two week event. Once the games are completed the use of this rail line may be very low. In Shanghai for the 2010 Expo some metro stations were opened that closed once the event concluded.

Governments are almost always the ones approving the construction a rail system, and it is within their power to not only approve the construction of the rail line but add facilities along the way next to the rail line. Developers and inhabitants will be keen to live alongside a rail system with a good quality service, and so interest in building new facilities along the rail corridor will normally be strong. In some cases the level of interest can be so high that the permission to build can attract substantial fees from developers, and these can be used to offset the cost of construction of the rail line. Government need not build the facility, this can be left to the private sector, and high quality rail projects often contain this type of project.

Governments can encourage the construction of additional facilities through zoning the land to whatever use is needed, and then approving the development application once it is received. In large cities the approval of a development application is a valuable thing, which can be used to encourage investment in the rail system.

In many instances the approval to allow the construction of a new apartment building or shopping may significantly change the character of an area. Land use policy here is very important in deciding what facilities to put where, and most governments will have a land use policy for any major town or city. This policy should be instrumental in deciding what facilities to put where.

The additional of facilities to a station changes the design of the station in a number of ways. These include:
- The station is larger to accommodate the additional passengers
- There are connections between the facility and the station, typically passenger walkways
- Passenger information needs to be focused on providing information on the nearby facility, such as directions, opening hours, etc
- Where the nearby facility has strong branding, such as a Disney amusement park, the colours of the station may be changed to reflect the colours of the facility.
- The nearby facility may need to be located at a specific spot, and the station may need to move to be closer to the facility

So what can be added to a station? There are many different types, and the list below is not intended to be exhaustive. Some of the different types of facility are:
- Shopping centres and department stores
- Airports
- Racecourses (usually for horses, but sometimes for dogs)
- Carparks
- Night markets (the ones in Taipei are a good example)
- Stadia (stadiums)
- Sporting facilities
- Cruise (ocean or rail) terminals
- Universities
- Theme parks
- Exhibition centres

Really anything can be connected that people might want to access. Another example not included in the above list would be a museum, or maybe even a park or scenic area. Hotels cam also be connected, but do not generate the same passenger numbers as the other facilities above.

Once built the shopping centre of apartment block needs to be within easy reach of any passenger station. This connection, mostly pedestrian, is very important, and there are right and wrong ways to create connections between different facilities and stations. Done right adding connections to important facilities to a rail system is a powerful way to increase revenue and the number of people using the system. Done incorrectly then few people will use any connections, and trains will run empty. As a general statement, any connection between the rail system and another centre or facility needs to be easily made and not take too long. Some of the problems that can be encountered include:
- The distance between the station and facility is too great to be practical
- There are too many stairs connecting the station and the centre, or the interchanges are poor
- The signage directing passengers from the station to the facility and vice versa is poor
- There are roads or other obstruction between the station and the facility
- Pedestrian connections are not covered and so passengers are exposed to the weather

Discussed below are some of the facilities that might be added to a rail line. Each one of these facilities has different strengths, but all add to the effectiveness of the railway and the quality of the station environment.

Shopping Centres

Shopping centres are commonly joined to rail stations. They are often placed over the top of the station, with the railway lines underneath, but underground malls connected to underground rail stations are also common. Rarely railway lines are built in elevated viaducts and some shops are underneath. The size of the shopping centre connected to the station varies from small one to very large multiple connected shopping centres.

Adding shops to a station provides numerous benefits, the most important of which is that passengers can now buy what they need from within the station precinct. The distinction should be made here between small shops such as bakeries and banks, and large department stores. Both can be added to stations, bakeries can be inside the station, but a department store would be located alongside the rail line due to its size. Small shops, convenience stores and banks, increase the amenity provided through the presence of the station. Passengers can buy items that they might need on their way to and from the station.

Large department stores alongside stations increase the number of passengers using that station. On major shopping days, such as big sales, it is possible to get people to and from shops quickly. In a city environment where there is a strong need to discourage the use of cars, providing shopping at stations is almost essential, as it eliminates the need for private journeys from a person's home to a shopping centre to buy food and other groceries.

In Hong Kong many stations contain at least:
- A bakery
- A bank, or at least an ATM
- At least one convenience store
- A take away shop with cheaply priced food

Another benefit from adding shops to stations is the railway can own the building and the space where the shop is located, and earn rental income. This income can be so large that it can make an otherwise unprofitable railway profitable. In cities where the rental cost is extremely high, this can be an important source of income for a railway. This is commonly done with commuter railways in Japan.

The photo below was taken in Taipei, and in the centre of the photo are ticket barriers for a station, and beyond this is Sogo department store. The distance between the shopping centre and the exit of the station is tiny, perhaps only 10 metres. Designing stations this way is a good way to generate passenger trips, and add convenience to the rail system.

Station Built Alongside a Large Department Store

Another additional benefit of shopping centres and shops in stations is security. Passengers feel secure and safe when exiting from a station to a brightly lit area where there are many people and shops. Wealthy and profitable shopping centres will have their own security force, and this can be used to protect passengers on the train system. This is one effective way of reducing the cost of providing security to passengers.

Airports

Airports are another major facility that are often connected by rail systems. Airports, especially international ones, are commonly far away from major cities, as the noise from aircraft taking off and landing is too loud for the airport to be placed close to the centre of the city. Providing transport to airports is very important for large cities, and one way is to connect the rail system to the airport.

The photo below is of the commuter train connecting Brisbane in Australia with the airport. This station is elevated.

An Airport Station

Connecting to the airport can often be very beneficial. There are however some problems. Airports move large numbers of people, but in comparison to a rail system, the number of people moved is not very large. For example a large airport might have no more than 50 landings and takeoffs per hour, with an average of 100 people in each plane. That's 5000 people per hour, which sounds like a lot, but in comparison to a rail system is actually a small number. Depending on the quality of other public transport to the airport, the rail system may not be highly used, and even very popular rail lines to airports are unlikely to fill entire trains with people. A large 8 car train can move one thousand people, so that's enough people for one train per hour in each direction, and only half full at that. The author's experience of airport trains is that they are mostly empty, and probably run at a loss.

Another facility that is sometimes provided is for check-in counters to be located at a railway station away from the airport, and customers check-in baggage before taking the airport express train. Passengers thus can avoid bring heavy luggage onto the train. Passengers will buy a ticket for the rail service before checking in baggage in the rail station. An example of this service is at Hong Kong station, where baggage can be checked in before catching the train to the airport.

Usually airports are connected to the rail system with a special train that is more comfortable and more expensive than normal metro trains. These trains are nicely fitted out, and often have televisions providing information to passengers on the sights and sounds of the city they are visiting. Also space is provided near the doors for passengers to put their luggage. This is particularly the case where the airport is a long way from the centre of the nearby city.

Sometimes rail systems are connected to the airport through the metro system or the suburban commuter rail system. This scenario is not as attractive as a specialised airport train, as luggage has to be manhandled onto and off metro trains, which can be very crowded. Hong Kong does not permit passengers to bring luggage above a certain size onto their metro trains, as they are too crowded and finding a spot for the luggage can be very challenging.

Carparks

Carparks have become somewhat standard in the construction of new commuter stations. Large carparks, which can store very large numbers of cars, can significantly add to the number of passengers that use the rail system. Most of the commuter carparks in Australia do not seem to charge any money for parking all day. Notwithstanding that they are very common, commuter carparks are not pretty thing, and are large somewhat unsightly concrete structures.

Carparks are unusual on metro stations, where thousands or tens of thousands of people are moving through the station. Carparks are typically provided for office workers to catch trains into the business centre of the city, work the day, and then catch the train out again and pick up their car from the car park. For trams, monorails, and light rail systems it would be unusual for large carparks to be built that cater entirely for the rail system. Light rail systems that extend from the centre of the city in the suburbs can have carparks located at stations, and this makes good sense in many cases.

Carparks are useful for commuter stations where people can drive to the station, park their car, and then catch the train into the city. The carpark will need to be large, and cars should not be constantly damaged and stolen. Also the roads leading in and out of the carpark should be wide and have the capacity to move the large number of people driving their cars into the carpark.

The carpark below is in western Sydney, and its purpose is to provide parking for the many passengers who catch the train from this station to the centre of the city to work.

Station with a Commuter Carpark

It should be kept in mind that people who drive to a commuter cark park are already in their cars, and they could just drive to work. It is better for the city if they don't as roads can become very congested, and the average travel speed on the roads will become quite low. A powerful incentive is needed to encourage people to get out of their cars and into trains. At the very least the rail service should be fast and frequent, and people should be able to get to work much faster by train than by car. The average speed of commuter rail services will need to be at least 50kms/hr, otherwise the service will be too slow. Also, to be successful a large carpark next to a station needs to be free or almost free.

It is easy to distinguish commuter and metro station from each other as the commuter stations will have carparks (as well as being different in other key ways).

Stadia/Stadiums

A stadium is a place where people go to watch large events, often sporting events, but also music concerts. Stadia are often located in the suburbs of large cities, but not outside the city itself. It is often very desirable for the rail system to connect to a large stadium, as a large stadium may be able to seat 80,000 people, or even more. Such large numbers of people are difficult to manage, and clearly it is impossible for everyone to drive to such a large sporting event.

Providing a rail connection to a large stadium can be one way to manage large crowds. Consider that most trains have a capacity of below 1000 people, and a metro train will be limited to maybe 2000 people per train, so the entire attending crowd of the stadium cannot be moved on a train, but many of them can. A large crowd of 100,000 people is very difficult to cater for, but a rail system can be very beneficial in managing these people.

A popular stadium may be used very frequently for many events, some with large crowds, but many with much smaller attendances, and so a rail connection can be very useful. In any large city there are likely to be many events of 10,000 to 20,000 people, and for these events the rail system normally manages quite well.

Transit Centres

Transit centres are places where people can change from one mode of transport to another. The term is also used to apply to bus stations where people can change from one bus line to another. This term can also apply to a rail to bus interchange, where people can move either to of from a bus and get on a train. Some bus transit centres can be very large, and hundreds of buses can move in to out of the centre on any given day.

Even in large cities with well developed rail systems, buses can be heavily patronised, and used extensively. A little known fact is that buses in Hong Kong are the dominant form of transportation, and move the largest number of people of any transport mode, despite the presence of an excellent metro system. Train lines can move very large numbers of people quickly, but there are always plenty of other destinations that require a bus connection. Buses are cheaper to buy and manage than trains, and are very useful for connections to places that don't require the same capacity as trains. Ticket prices for buses are also cheaper (or should be), so providing bus services in a city in addition to train service can allow those cities with less money the opportunity to spend less on transport. All of this means that bus-rail connections are a common thing in a well planned city.

The photo below was taken at the bus transit centre at Southern Cross station in Melbourne in Australia. This is probably the largest transit centre in Australia, and the reader may notice that the photo has a sign with the number "56", which is the by number, so there are at least 56 bays, assuming that the bay numbers start at 1 and don't skip any numbers. The bus shown in the photo has the VLine logo on it, and this is the regional rail company in Victoria, so this bus is owned by a rail company.

Bus Transit Centre Under a Station

Also common are rail connections to transit centres where coaches arrive and depart. Coaches are different from buses in that they are designed for long distance transport, and have toilet and luggage facilities. Coaches can have many features in common with aircraft, such as tray tables, and televisions displaying movies. Air conditioning is common on coach travel in Australia.

Coaches in many cities depart and arrive from a transit centre. As most destinations are only serviced once per day, people need to wait until the departure time of their coach service. This type of transit centre is common in Australia, and typically facilities are provided such as lockers, showers and toilets, budget accommodation, as well as ticket sales counters for the major bus companies. A well designed transit centre will have a rail station nearby, so that visiting tourists and others can make their way from the rail system to the coach terminal and catch their coach to its destination. A particularly good combination occurs when the rail system connects both the airport and the coach transit centre.

As with any rail connections to other transport, it is important that there are frequent and reliable services to transit centres. People often get stressed with rushing for connections, especially if the next leg of their journey is long or expensive, and the coach only departs once per day. Delays have a very large impact upon this type of travel, as once a connection is missed, the cost of buying a new ticket can be very large.

Universities

Rail systems often connect with universities. University students often don't have much money, and often do not own a vehicle. They often live at home with their parents, and travel long distances to get to university. Despite this in South East Asia, and Australia, this type of transport connection is actually quite uncommon, and even in Hong Kong the metro system rarely connects to any major university. Having said this since a station has opened at Hong Kong University in 2014.

Connecting universities to rail transportation can make a lot of sense. Large universities may have over twenty thousand students, and on any given day maybe half actually attend university. As most students will arrive in the morning, rail services to the university will run with substantial numbers of paying passengers. Other passengers on the rail system will include employees of the university, also a large number of people, and people who also live nearby the university. The population density nearby universities can be very high, as students move there to be close to the university, and don't earn much as they are young and have yet to work. Overall, rail services to universities, where they exist, are well patronised.

One problem with providing rail services to universities is the size of the uni. Many universities in Australia are extremely large, and walking from one side to another may take over half an hour. Care needs to be exercised that the station is placed in a location where students can access the university. Where the university is too far from the station, the university may provide a bus between the station and the university, but passenger numbers will be a lot lower. A station connecting a university needs to be very close to the university itself, and within 10 minutes walk of most of the major buildings within the university, such as the business faculty or the library.

Theme Parks/Amusement Park

A theme park is a place where people go to enjoy themselves, often with their children, which has a common idea that connects the many ideas together. Theme parks need large numbers of people to be profitable, as they cost a lot to build and operate. Disneyland is probably the best known chain of amusement parks, and there are many others scattered around the world.

Rail systems can connect to the theme park, but in many cases there are small trains that move around the theme park. These small trains are really tourist trains, and have a very limited capacity. Nonetheless, they are real train systems, despite their small size.

Disneyland in Hong Kong has a special purpose rail line connecting the rail system to one of the metro lines. This rail line, a full metro line with the same capacity as other metro lines in Hong Kong, was constructed to connect the theme part to the rest of the rail system, and its construction was part of the cost of construction of the overall park.

In Australia a large number of theme parts have gone out of business. Theme parks have very high operational costs, and only a very successful theme part can stay in business. It would be very embarrassing if a rail line is built to a theme park, at great expense, only for the theme park to shut down. Notwithstanding the risk associated with connecting theme parks to the main rail system, where the theme park is very successful then this is a good way of increasing the number of passengers.

The photo below is of the specialised train that connects the rail system to the amusement park in Hong Kong. Notice the Mickey Mouse shaped windows on the train.

Hong Kong Disney Train

Exhibitions Centres/Conference Centres

Exhibition centres are places where businesses can have an exhibition to show their wares, and display to the world what can be bought. There are exhibitions on a large number of different products, cars are a very popular item to display, but there are many others, such as jewellery, travel, boats, and many others. Large cities have a constant stream of different exhibitions, and they can be very popular. The rail industry also has exhibitions, where all the different types of products for sale to build a railway are displayed. Some of the information used to write this book was sourced from exhibitions of this type.

Whilst many of these exhibitions are closed to the general public, many are not. Those that are closed to the public may have much smaller attendances than those open to the public. Large exhibitions may have tens of thousands of visitors. As with any other event that generates large numbers of visitors, a rail connection is desirable because it can move people to the exhibition without congesting the roads around the exhibition. Twenty thousand people per day can normally be easily accommodated by a rail system, and this would be a typical number for a large exhibition.

The photo below shows the exhibition centre in Singapore, with a train in the station behind the exhibition centre. As with almost all the public transport in Singapore, again this design is very good, with a very good and easy connection between the station and the exhibition centre. The only criticism that can be levelled at Singapore with its exhibition centre is that it is in a very quiet and unremarkable part of the city. Exhibition centres in Australia tend to be located in very flashy and prestigious parts of the city, somewhere that is very interested to walk out of the centre and see, which is not the case in Singapore. Nonetheless the transport connection is very good.

Train Station next to an Exhibition Centre

Conferences have become increasing common around the world, and these events are usually open to those in specific industries. Conferences are events where guest speakers present to people from a specific industry. Large conferences can attract tens of thousands of attendees.

Conferences can be just as successful as large exhibitions. Conference centres are often co-located with exhibition centres, but there is no reason why the two different types of facilities need to be at the same place.

Racecourses and other sporting event places

Racecourses are found throughout the world, but are particularly common in Australia with almost every major town possessing one. In major cities in Australia there are almost always several racecourses, and attendances at horse races is very high. Rail connections to racecourses in Australia is the norm, and almost all racecourses in Sydney, and other major cities, have special purpose built stations for use at those racecourses. These stations are opened only for race days, which are surprisingly common.

The station below is for Rosehill Racecourse, which is for horse racing. The station is at the front, and at the back is the racecourse. If the reader looks carefully, the green doors under the name Rosehill Gardens is actually the entry point to the racecourse. Notice that the platform is large and quite wide. Also interestingly there are two sets of fences, which allow the waiting crowd to wait whilst the train is approaching.

Station next to a Racecourse

Rail systems can be extended to many different venues, such as speedways, Olympic pools, and any other sporting venue. Sydney hosted the 2000 Olympic games, and there is a rail connection into the centre of the Olympic sports centre. This rail connection has been used for a large number of events.

Major Tourist Attractions

Major tourist attractions can bring large numbers of passengers to a city. Passenger numbers swell on hot days, and weekends and public holidays. Particularly famous tourist attractions can have tens of thousands of visitors on any given day, and it is very beneficial to the economy of the region to have large numbers of people spend money.

The tourist attraction may be connected through a special purpose tourist railway, or it may be connected through a normal connection into a metro or other more standard type rail system. There is no special rail connection into Notre Dame in Paris, it is connected to the rail system through the metro, as with much of the city of Paris. Either way, connecting high value tourist attractions to a rail systems makes a lot of sense.

The photo below is of the train to Versailles in Paris. Note the very unusual ceiling, and the train that goes to the old king's palace has special decorations on the ceiling, which are representative of the place the tourists are going to. The interior of this train was beautiful to look at, and really did give the viewer a feel for the palace they were going to visit. Trains to Versailles seem to be very busy, and move large numbers of people.

The Tourist Train To Versailles

Note this train is a double decker train, and from what can be seen by the casual observer, is no different to the other double decker trains in Paris other than the richly decorated interior.

REFERENCES

1. Cervero, R. & Murakami, J. *Rail and Property Development in Hong Kong: Experiences and Extensions*, Urban Studies, 2009 46:2019 Aug 2009

2. HKSAR Government *Hong Kong the Facts: Tourism*, http://www.tourism.gov.hk

Chapter 9 Underground Stations

No discussion of rail stations would be complete without covering underground stations. Around the world there are hundreds if not thousands of these, and many of the most important stations in many countries are underground. Underground stations are used where the rail line itself is underground, and passengers walk from the surface to the rail line below.

The construction of stations is also a large part of the cost of building any new rail line, especially where the station are underground. They are a point where many of the engineering systems involved with running are passenger railway are installed and operated, and so many station are often very infrastructure intensive. Whilst the public may not see it, most stations contain many unseen rooms where large numbers of equipment items are sitting humming away. This is particularly so for underground stations, which are even more complex, and have more infrastructure installed.

Underground stations are expensive to construct, require a lot of infrastructure, so are very equipment intensive. Underground stations also present significant safety risks, as any smoke evolved from a station can potentially accumulate there and injure or kill anyone who cannot be evacuated. Care must be exercised in the design of any station to ensure it is correctly designed, and does not create and safety or passenger movement problems.

Another challenge exists with large metro systems with very large numbers of passenger movements. The aim is to get people on and off trains as quickly as possible, and passengers lingering in the station will cause trains waiting on the platform to be delayed as passengers cannot board or alight. The large numbers of people mean that any blockage to passenger flow can have a very large and adverse effect to the speed at which people can board and alight trains, and to the dwell time.

It should be remembered that many types of station do not have large movements of passengers. Many publications and conference papers seem to assume that all stations have large passenger flows. It is certainly true that the larger stations are the more significant ones, and will have larger passenger flows. These ones, and this is mostly metro stations, need to be designed carefully so that passengers can move through the station quickly and effectively. In very busy metro stations, the number of people passing through the station can be extremely large, and so correctly designing the station is very important. Stations with small passenger movements, and there are very large numbers of these around the world, are far easier to design and build. This is especially so where the station is at ground level. The design challenge with stations with small numbers of passenger movements is far lower than for busy stations.

The question arises of what exactly constitutes an underground station. A station may be partially underground, and be built on a hill or cutting, so that it appears to be underground, or may be partially underground. Stations can have shopping centres built over them, so that they appear to be underground, but actually are above or at ground level. In some cases a station may be constructed at the top of a hill, and so is underground, but at each end of the station is a portal where the rail line moves out from underground, and so the only part of the rail line that is underground is the station. In Sydney Kings Cross station is designed this way, where at each end of the station there is a portal, and the rail line at both ends of the station is above ground.

Whilst a search for any references failed to reveal anything that discussed what the definition for an underground station is, the following observations can be made:
- Stations located deep underground will always be defined as being underground
- Stations where the rail line is buried for some distance either side of the station can be considered as being underground
- Stations which are above ground, but covered by a shopping centre, can in some cases be considered to be an underground station, especially where the rail lines at either end of the station are also underground
- Elevated stations, which are above ground, may appear to the travelling public to be below ground, but should always considered above ground stations
- Stations with one or more sides exposed, which are not walls or tunnels, are clearly not underground stations
- Any station where a passenger can look up and see the sky, without looking through a roof or other structure is probably not an underground station

Perhaps the best rule to use is if, from any part of the station it is impossible for any passenger standing on a platform to see natural sunlight, for any part of the day, then the station can be considered to be an underground station. Applying this rule would exclude a large number of stations, such as Taoyuan station in Taiwan, on the high speed rail system, where sunlight is clearly visible at one end of the station for most of the day. It is suggested that the definition for underground stations be interpreted fairly strictly, so as to limit the number of stations defined as being underground.

Ordinarily freight trains are not permitted to pass through underground stations that service passengers. The mixing of freight and passenger services has a profound effect on the design of any rail line, and this is especially so for underground stations and rail lines. Freight trains are often fuelled with diesel, and this is a combustible fuel, and even though it is difficult for it to catch fire, it will under the right circumstances. Diesel motors can explode if poorly maintained, so extreme care must be taken if freight trains are permitted through underground stations. Often freight will be banned from passing through any underground rail station with passengers, but potentially in some cases it may be required to allow freight to pass through underground station. An alternative solution may be to restrict the freight trains to particular times of the day when passenger trains do not operate. In Australia there are no underground stations where freight is permitted to pass through at all.

Another consideration with underground stations is how to manage passengers when they become ill. This seems to be more and more common lately, certainly in Australia where the population is aging, and passengers can become ill on trains and then be moved from the train to the platform. Underground stations can be so deep below ground that it may be difficult or near impossible to get passengers out when they become ill. This is especially the case for stations with no lifts, which is not uncommon, even for underground stations. Some passengers can be very heavy, and not that easy to remove or assist from the station, so some care needs to be exercised in deciding how to get ill passengers from platforms. We can also note that almost all stations will not have a lift operating all the way from the unpaid surface to paid platforms deep below ground, and so as a minimum 2 lifts are needed to get an ill passenger to the surface to be met by an ambulance. The need to be able to evacuate sick passengers is a complication to the fire and life safety design required for stations.

Fire Protection and Safety for Underground Stations

Underground stations are an enclosed and confined space. If a fire starts in an underground station then the smoke can accumulate very rapidly, and present an extremely serious risk to anyone still in the station. Smoke can rapidly accumulate and cause damage to the lungs of anyone present, and so smoke management is an important part of station design.

Large fires in an underground station are very serious. Apart from the risk of the smoke, what can make fires so dangerous is the speed with which they can grow. Small fires can become large fires very quickly if there is enough material and oxygen. The fast growth rates of fires means that once a fire starts there is very little time to evacuate passengers from both rollingstock or from platforms, and designing stations to allow rapid egress is very important.

The main defence against fires in underground stations is removing any possible fuel source. Materials used in the construction of a station should be highly resistant to catching fire, and not burn unless heated to a very high temperature. All materials will burn if the temperature is high enough, so it is not possible to find a material that is completely resistant to fire. Fire resistant materials should also be resistant to structural collapse as long as possible when exposed to a fire, and the longer the better. Structural collapse in an underground station would be very serious were it to ever happen.

In the construction of any station, fire hardening is very important, almost all railways will construct their stations to be as fire resistant as possible. Other mitigations for fires in underground stations include escape and exit from the station, and whilst not as important as fire hardening the station and rollingstock, and also not as important as stopping the fire starting in the first place, it also important and needs to be considered.

Electrical wiring in a station also needs to be a very good quality, as fire can start when problems occur in the wiring. Electricity has the capability, especially where the cabling has short circuits or bare wiring, to start fires. To protect against this special wiring is used that is more fire resistant, and less likely to fray or become bare and have the potential to start a fire.

Large fires are fortunately very rare in almost all modern rail systems. Small fires, especially in some countries, are commonly started by vandals and school children as pranks, and can be quite common. To prevent these minor incidents becoming very major, it is important for any rail system to ensure that fire hardened materials are used in stations and for rollingstock. A small fire started by an 11 year old school student should never be allowed to become a raging inferno, and the use of poor quality materials can allow this to happen.

An important standard for the design of stations is NFPA 130, Standard for Fixed Guideway Transit and Passenger Rail Systems. It is a standard for the US for the design of rail systems, and it focuses on the safety and fire related aspects of station and rail tunnel design. Produced by the National Fire Protection Association in the US, it contains many proscriptive requirements for the design of underground stations. This standard is used and followed extensively in the US and Asia, but not in Europe, where European Union and national standards are used.

NFPA 130 discusses a number of topics, and this includes chapter 2 on the design of underground stations. In this chapter are some requirements on materials for underground stations, fire protection of staff and other areas, but also three requirements that are used extensively in station design. These are:
- Platforms must be able to be evacuated in 4 minutes or less (but not necessarily out of the station)
- The entire station should be capable of being evacuated in 6 minutes or less
- The maximum distance from any point on a platform to an exit should be no greater than 300 feet (or 91.4 metres)

The standard also provides for estimating the number of people that should be used for any simulation of the escape time from the station. This is based on the capacity of trains entering the station for each platform, and the number of people that might be waiting to board a train, multiplied by a safety factor, commonly 2. The modelling of the design of the station then involves estimating how long the station takes to evacuate, and a compliant design can evacuate passengers in less than the required time.

The use of NFPA 130 seems to be popular in Asia and Australia, and is obviously common in North America. It is also used in South America. It is not mandatory in Asia or Australia at all, and has no legal force, but seems to be popular because of its clear and easy to understand rules on what is acceptable or not. Commonly a station that is designed to NFPA 130 will have a number of easy to reach exits, which are quite wide that can accommodate large numbers of people. A long platform such as 300 metres long will have at least 4 exits, and each will be designed to allow a lot of people to pass through.

NFPA 130 also contains the provision that the entire station must be evacuated in 6 minutes or less. This means that there needs to be enough room for people to move quickly from the paid to the unpaid area. Turnstiles and barriers are common in most stations, to stop fare evaders from entering the paid area without a ticket, but in times of emergency they can impede the flow of passengers exiting the station. Consider that a metro station will typically have at least 2 platforms, and each metro train can typically take up to 3000 people, so a design load of 9000 people for an emergency is not unreasonable. They will need to be able to exit the station quickly, and through barriers and turnstiles. NFPA provides that a typical number for the people per minute that can move through a turnstile is 25, so that means a large metro station will require at least 60 turnstiles. That's an extremely large number, and unlikely to be implemented in practice, so another solution is necessary.

In some rail systems there are alternative exits and staircases available for passengers in the event of a fire. These hidden staircases are only available when a fire emergency starts, and there is a need to evacuate the station. As most metro stations are very busy, and have large numbers of passengers, it is not surprising that in an emergency it is not possible to evacuate the station in the time required under NFPA130. A solution to this is to provide another entirely separate set of staircases, much like fire escapes in large buildings, but with some differences. These exits are controlled by the fire alarm system, and are not accessible unless there is some sort of emergency. They also have no barriers, or turnstiles, as this would slow the movement of passengers out of the station. Another interesting feature of these "secret" exits is that they only need to connect the platform to a place where passengers can exit safely, and this may include another part of the station. Typically these exits connect the platform area to the concourse of a station, but outside of the paid area, so that passenger escape is not limited by difficult to move through barriers.

Research has found that people fleeing a fire will not attempt to escape through an exit that is obscured by smoke. This is even the case where that exit is the only safe way to escape a fire. For this reason a major focus of any underground station design is to ensure that any exit identified for escape from a fire should be ventilated sufficiently that smoke cannot accumulate there to appear to block the exit. This often means that there should be large air-conditioning ducts located close to the exit to clear any smoke, and this needs to be considered when constructing the station.

The cost of management and construction of an underground station is much higher than for above ground stations. Above ground stations have a much lower risk profile, and this translates into lower operating and maintenance costs. Underground stations require complex fire protection and ventilation systems, which make them much more expensive to build, and need to be monitored. Complex ventilation systems need to be maintained, and the need to be supervised in a control centre somewhere. Again, this all adds costs.

Modelling of smoke flow in a station is very important, as this allows analysis of the safe places in the station, the correct means of escape, and how large a fire needs to be before there are fatalities. These types of models are commonly reported on in journals and conference papers, and often have three dimensional models of stations where smoke moves outwards from a large fire. In the models fires are almost always placed in trains stopped at the stations, and small to large fires are modelled. The amount of smoke evolved from a fire of different sizes is estimated, and then the smoke allowed to flow through the station to see what happens.

Particularly complex models can allow for the movement of passengers through the station, moving away from the smoke. The intention is that passengers can escape the fire without too much difficulty. It should be noted that a very large fire is difficult for passengers to escape from, and even the best designed underground station will have difficulty in protecting passengers. The types of things that the modelling is looking for is:
- Can small fires cause fatalities?

- Will the design of the station cause people to be trapped if the fire is in specific unlucky locations?
- Are slow moving passengers unable to escape even small fires?
- Does smoke moves in an unpredictable way, and traps people in an unexpected part of the station?
- If the station is safe during non-peak times, is it more dangerous during peak times when the passenger load is larger?

Should fire and life safety modelling of a station reveal any of these problems then the station will need to be redesigned. The redesign will then need to be modelled to ensure that any detected problems have been removed.

Infrastructure in an Underground Station

With many of the engineering systems installed into rail tunnels, some support systems are needed sitting on stations to support the equipment in tunnels. In practice this means that underground stations are much larger than just the space needed for passengers. There are all sorts of equipment rooms necessary to keep equipment operating. Stations are a convenient place to put all of this equipment, and without a station sometimes a service centre needs to be installed into a rail line. A service centre has many of the features of a station, but is not accessible to the public. In Sydney there is one such centre at present, with another being constructed.

The design of underground stations needs to consider all the additional equipment and space needed to install the equipment. As the provision of space underground is expensive, it's unfortunate that so much additional space is needed for all this other equipment. This make the cost of constructing an underground station even higher, and it was expensive to begin with. The author has seen plans of stations where the equipment rooms needed represented over 50% of the total floor space of a station, and the public areas were quite large. The ventilation in particular takes up a lot of space. Some of the different types of equipment rooms installed into an underground station include:
- A control room
- Ventilation rooms
- Fire control rooms
- Water treatment plant
- Substations (power rooms)

- Communications rooms
- Water pumping stations

Each of the rooms listed above comes with a substantial cost, and needs to be clearly identified. Maintainers will need access to these rooms, as will emergency services and police in the event of any emergency. The number and size of these can have a powerful effect on the cost of a rail tunnel.

Ventilation in a rail tunnel is installed for two reasons; providing fresh air, and managing smoke in an emergency. Ventilation is created using pumps, which can move air at high speed. Connected to the pumps are air conditioning ducts, sometimes called HVAC (High Velocity Air Conditioning). The pumps push the air through the ducts to where it is needed.

Along with the ducts and pumps come flow meters, pressure gauges, and temperature sensors. These are quite useful, and are used to monitor the flow of air. These meters and gauges are connected to the control room, so the control room operator can see what air is moving, and where to, and what temperature it is. Air conditioning systems in underground tunnels usually work quite well, and provide very few problems.

All the ventilation equipment is normally contained within a room, often located in underground stations. These rooms are sometimes called ventilation rooms. Depending on the design of the tunnel, the need for fresh air, etc, one or two ventilation rooms are needed in each location. As with any infrastructure, keeping the amount needed to a minimum is the key to efficient construction and maintenance.

Tunnels and the related infrastructure can also have a control room, where operators are assigned to monitor the tunnel. This is a pretty boring job, as very little happens and they are there for emergencies. The control room has visibility over the different engineering systems, what is happening, and the movement of trains. Control rooms for tunnels performa different function to controlling train movements. The function of controlling the movement of trains may be near by, or even located in the same room, but the function is different to managing a rail tunnel. The role of the computer system that oversees the control room is a little controversial, as some favour a high level of involvement for any automatic system, and others prefer the operators to make decisions on what should happen in the event of an emergency.

A control room is a place where a number of operators sit and watch screens all day. Often very dark, operators seem to like to sit in relative darkness to watch screens. The control room is connected to all the various different systems, and if a problem occurs on any of them, then the computer system generates an alarm. An alarm is both an audible alarm, as well as something on the screen designed to catch the eye of the operator. If a fire starts in the tunnel, then alarms will start sounding from the control panel.

From day to day very little happens in tunnels, and incidents are rare. From the perspective of the rail system design, one control room can monitor hundreds of kilometres of tunnel before they require a second person. A very bad thing to do is create a short tunnel that requires a control room, with very little to do, because a control room is expensive, and it's bad practise to create one for a short rail tunnel. It's best, where there are several rail tunnels in close proximity to one another, to combine all the control rooms into a single room which monitors them all.

Many rail tunnels provide something called "escape". It is considered desirable in many countries that if there is an emergency in a tunnel, then passengers have a reasonable chance to flee the area, and escape should be provided. Escape usually means walkways down the side of the rail tunnel, which increases the size of the tunnel, and hence it's cost. Escape is also the reason why twin bore rail tunnels are used instead of single bore, as passengers can escape down one of the tunnels and leave the tunnel with the emergency in it. Having twin bore tunnels is extremely expensive, and should be done only when there is a clear need to do so.

A communications room is the place where all the information on what is happening in the tunnel is relayed back to the control room, and potentially other locations where the tunnel is monitored. The local fire brigade may be given some monitoring over the tunnel, especially if the tunnel is in a metropolitan area. Also security companies may monitor doors and access to the tunnel, and respond where someone has accessed the facility and not been authorised to do so. Communications rooms are full of banks of modems, switches, power supplies and cabling.

The fire control room is a room where the fire brigade, or similar organisation, can attend a fire emergency, and control the various systems in both underground tunnels and stations. The fire control room is located in a place where large vehicles can be parked, and where access is easy. The fire control room provides control over lifts and escalators, lighting, water and hydrants, as well as power. There may be many fire control rooms, for example, one at each station, and at any tunnel portals. That can be a large number.

A substation is a place where the power is provided to the station and tunnels. Incoming power is normally the wrong voltage for use in a station, so it needs to be converted to a more useful voltage. This room is sometimes called the power room. Inside the substation are transformers and busbars that allow power to be distributed to the different pieces of equipment that require power. The placement of a substation can be very important, because occasionally substations catch fire, and so this risk needs to be managed. As substations are potential sources of fire, they would never be placed in the middle of an island platform surrounded by passengers, unless there was simply no other option.

REFERENCES

1. Zhang, C. & Li, L. Zhang, D. & Zhang, S. *Types and Characteristics of Safety Accidents Induced by Metro Construction*, 2009 International Conference on Information Management, Innovation Management and Industrial Engineering, 209

2. Chief Fire and Rescue Advisor *GRA 4.2 Incidents involving transport systems - rail*, Communities and Local Government Fire and Rescue Service Operational Guide, 2011

3. NFPA130 2000, *Standard for Fixed Guideway Transit and Passenger Rail Systems*, 2000 Edition

4. Rail Accident Investigation Branch *Technical Investigation Report concerning the Fire on Eurotunnel Freight Shuttle 7412 on September 2008*, November 2010 (in French)

5. Krasyuk, A. *Calculation of Tunnel Ventilation in Shallow Subways*, Journal of Mining Science, Vol 41, No 3, 2005

6. Efron N, & Read, N *Analysing International Tunnel Costs*, Worcester Polytechnic Institute, Feb 2012

7. ARUP Burnley Tunnel Fire – The ARUP View, April 2007, http://www.index-files.com/file-pdf/burnley-tunnel-fire-the-arup-view-tunnel-details

8. Zuber, P. *Compared Safety Features for Rail Tunnels* First International Symposium, Prague 2004, Safe and Reliable Tunnels. Innovation European Achievements

9. Woods, E. *Bored Tunnels*, The Arup Journal, 1/2004

10. Twine, D. *Cut-and-Cover Tunnels* The Arup Journal, 1/2004

11. Tarada, F. *Critical Velocities for Smoke Control in Tunnel Cross-Passages*, First International Conference on Major Tunnel and Infrastructure Projects, May 2000, Taiwan

12. Smith, G. & Ceranic, B. *Spatial Layout Planning in Sub-Surface Rail Station Design for Effective Fire Evacuation*, Architectural Engineering and Design Management, 2008, Volume 4, Pages 99 – 120

13. Ghiasi, V. et al *Design Criteria of Subway Tunnels* Australian Journal of Basic and Applied Sciences, 4(12): 5894-5907, 2010

14. European Parliament *Assessment of the Safety of Tunnels Study*, (IP/A/STOA/FWC/2005-28/SC22/29)

15. Ghiasi, V. et al *Construction Regulations along Metro Alignment*, Australian Journal of Basic and Applied Sciences, 4(12): 5972-6009, 2010

16. GHD Pty Ltd, *The Design of the Lane Cove River Cut and Cover Tunnels and Cofferdam for the Epping to Chatswood Rail Line*, ASEC Conference, 2005

17. European Union, *Directive 2001/16/EC/ - Draft Technical Specification for Interoperability: Aspect Safety in Rail Tunnels*

18. Thamm, B. *The new EU Directive on Road and Tunnel Safety*, International Symposium on Tunnel Safety and Security, November 2004

19. Bopp, R & Hagennah, B. Aerodynamics, Ventilation and Tunnel Safety for High Speed Rail Tunnels, http://paginas.fe.up.pt/~hsrt/documents/RudolfBopp_abs_001.pdf

20. Miclea, P. et al *International Tunnel Fire-Safety Design Practices*, Ashrae Journal, Aug 2007

21. Queensland Co-ordinator General Northern Link Road Tunnel, April 2010, http://www.statedevelopment.qld.gov.au/resources/project/legacy-way-project/northern-link-road-tunnel-cg-report.pdf

22. Klinger, R. *Radio Coverage for Road and Rail Tunnels in Tunnels in the Frequency Range 75 to 1000 MHz*, Vehicular Technology Conference, 1991.

23. Hewitt, P. *Groundwater Control for Sydney Rock Tunnels*, AGS AUCTA Mini-Symposium: Geotechnical Aspects of Tunneling for Infrastructure Projects, Oct 2005

24. Quqing, G. *Metro Tunnelling in China*, Tunnelling and Underground Space Technology, Vol 5, No 3, pp 271 – 275, 1990

25. Gabay, D. *Compared Fire Safety Features for Metro Tunnels*, Safe and Reliable Tunnels, First International Symposium, Prague 2004

26. Soons, C.J. et al *Framework of a quantitative risk analysis fore the fire safety in metro systems*, Tunnelling and Underground Space Technology 21 (2006) 281

27. Beard, A. *Tunnel safety, risk assessment and decision-making*, Tunnelling and Underground Space Technology, 25 (2010) 91 – 94

28. Muller, M. Tunnel Safety; where we are now, http://www.imia.com/wp-content/uploads/2013/05/EP22-2005-Tunnel-Safety-Where-are-we-now.pdf

29. OECD Norway Tunnel Safety, 2006, http://www.oecd.org/norway/36100776.pdf

30. Yoon SW, & Choi, H. *Development of Quantitative Risk Analysis Tool for the Fire Safety in Railway Tunnel*, International Forum on Decision Making, Japan May 2009

31. Williams, R. & Chalmers, G. *Recent Developments in the Design of Cut and Cover Construction for Railway Tunnels and Stations*, Conference on Railway Engineering, Adelaide, May 2000

32. Krenn, F. et al *Shallow Tunnelling in Soft Ground – Influence of the Chosen Support System on the System Behaviour*, Geomechanik und Tunnelbau 1 (2008), Heft 3

33. Cheong, SW. *Fire Safety Design for Rapid Transit Systems*, Proceedings of the international conference, Fire India, 2004

34. Tarada, F. & King, M. *Structural Fire Protection of Railway Tunnels*, Railway Engineering Conference, University of Westminster, UK, June 2009

35. Wagner, H. *The Governance of Cost in Tunnel Design and Construction*, 1 Congresso Brasilero de Tuneis e Estruturas Subterraneas Seminario Internacional South American Tunnelling

36. Neumann, C. et al Koralm Tunnel – Development of Tunnel System Design and Safety Concept, http://www.ilf.com/fileadmin/user_upload/publikationen/39_Koralm_Tunnel_Development_of_Tunnel_System_Design_and_Safety_Concept.pdf

37. United Nations Inland Transport Committee *Recommendations of the Multi-Disciplinary Group of Experts on Safety in Tunnels (Rail)*, TRANS/AC.9/9 Dec 2003

38. International Technology Scanning Program *Underground Transportation Systems in Europe: Safety, Operations, and Emergency Response*, FHWA-PL-06-016, June 2006

39. BHBB Cross City Tunnel Joint Venture *Construction Compliance Report for the Cross City Tunnel Project*, http://www.crosscity.com.au/files/documents/15_1st-environment-report-jan-july03.pdf

40. *The Handbook of Tunnel Fire Safety*, edited by Alan Beard and Richard Carvel, 2005

Chapter 10 Managing and Modelling Passenger Flows

Introduction

Some rail systems have very large numbers of passengers. Some metro stations move experience large passenger movements, for example, Mong Kok station in Hong Kong moves over 200,000 people per day. This level of passenger movements can create some real problems, and so the design of these stations is very important. The greater the passenger load through a busy station, the more important the design of the station becomes. Standard tools and process exist for designing stations, and these are discussed below.

Where stations are extremely busy, passengers may be unable to exit the station quickly, and when the subsequent train arrives then passengers may not be able to alight from the train quickly. This can slow down disembarkation, which results in the subsequent train have to wait while passengers attempt to alight. In severe cases, train movements may be severely disrupted, and the headway may grow significantly. Where a railway has invested heavily in improving the headway, this benefit can be lost where passenger overcrowding is so great that the better headway cannot be used.

In addition to the effect on train headways, passenger comfort is a very important factor in designing stations. Passengers do not like being cramped and crowded, and in a large station this can be a real problem. Some people dislike being touched by others, inadvertent or otherwise, and whilst people brushing against one another in a crowd is unavoidable, many people don't like it nonetheless. A slow exit from a station is in reality an increase in passenger travel times, and where travel times are too large then the public will not use the service. Severe overcrowding also provides the opportunity for all types of petty crime, such as pick pocketing and theft of bags, wallets and cameras. Also young girls and women may be touched in an inappropriate way, and so in general severe overcrowding should be avoided where possible.

Problems with passenger crowding typically arise in underground stations, but can also occur with above ground stations as well. Large metro stations are commonly seriously affected by overcrowding, as the numbers of people being moved can be very large and difficult to manage. More uncommonly, passenger crowding in tram systems can also be extremely severe, and the tiny platforms in the middle of streets provided for tram systems can be completely overwhelmed by large passenger movements. The tram systems in both Melbourne and Hong Kong suffer from extreme overcrowding, and in Hong Kong the tram service may be 2 or 3 times slower in peak times than on Sunday mornings. The small tram stops are insufficient in size for the number of people attempting to use them.

Light rail, HSR and regional rail systems seem less prone to overcrowding, as these systems may not have the same level of intensity of passenger movements. Also HSR and regional trains spend more time at platforms, and often have a large terminus where trains wait for the departure time, giving passenger plenty of opportunity to board the train. Commuter rail systems can suffer from severe overcrowding, but many of the services on these systems are relatively lightly loaded, and so severe overcrowding is uncommon.

In Japan and China rail services of almost any kind are overcrowded. In China regional services can suffer from severe overcrowding, and tickets are sold on long distance trains without seats, and passengers must stand for long journeys. Commuter trains in Japan are also very crowded, in addition to metro systems in big cities which are also often crowded.

In many cases managing overcrowding can be addressed with increasing the size of the station, at least within the station. Larger platforms, larger and more entrances and exits, and more barriers are clear and relatively straightforward solutions to overcrowding. The problem is that the space is not always available for platforms and walkways of very large size, or the cost of excavation of an underground station can be excessive. Trams systems may have very limited space because of the placement of stations in the middle of roads, and so cannot be increased in size without enormous difficulty. In many cases a compromise is needed to allow for stations that are not as large as needed, but can still cope with the passenger volumes predicted.

Smart station design can alleviate many overcrowding problems. Where space for a station is limited, use of the available space efficiently may present some interesting design challenges. One way to manage this situation is to create many different station designs, and then test them with modelling software to see which performs the best. The definition of best really means the rate at which passengers can exit the station, with the fastest being the best.

To get in and out of stations, walking is almost always required. Escalators assist with upwards and downwards movements, and moving walks are also used, but in almost every case at some point passengers need to walk to exit a station. Walking speeds vary enormously from person to person, and in lightly crowded spaces faster walkers will not be impeded. In heavily crowded spaces, the fast walkers will need to slow down, and in severely crowded spaces walking speeds are much slower. Modelling of the movement of passengers through stations involves estimating the speed of movement, with faster being better. Passenger speed will depend on their environment, crowding, the incline they are walking on, and a number of other factors. The rate of movement of people in different environments has been extensively studied, and fairly accurate and effective modelling of passenger exit speeds is possible.

Passenger Flow Modelling

Passenger movement speeds vary based on what they are walking on, in addition to a number of other factors. Some of the common structures that people must negotiate in a station includes:
- Stairs, both in and upward and downward direction
- Ramps
- Flat ground
- Escalators
- Moving walkways

People move substantially faster on flat ground than on stairs and ramps. This makes stairs and ramps the bottleneck for getting passengers on and off platforms, hence the focus they receive in the study of station design and managing dwell times.

Most basic calculations of estimating passenger exit speeds from a station are based on a flow rate. This is defined below.

f = *passenger flow per unit width of subway/walkway*
S = *passenger speed*
D = *passenger density*

So we can write:

$$f = S \times D$$

The flow rate of people per linear metre increases when their speed increased, or they are packed together more closely and so the density is higher. The passenger flow rate can then be used as follows:

Number of people moving through a corridor per minute = width of corridor x flow rate

The flow rate per unit width is often used for work with station design. Where crowding is heavy, and passenger movements slow, this can be accommodated by widening the available cross-sectional area to allow for more people. Widening corridors can be very effective, as this allows more people to flow through, and can increase the average speed as crowding is lower.

Notice that the flow rate is per unit width. Stations are a complex 2 dimensional design in many cases, but flow measurements are per unit width. This means that any modelling software will need to convert a station layout into a series of linear distances for which a flow calculation can be completed. In many cases this is relatively straight forward, but in others can be very difficult, especially where there are many different entrances and exits. Consider the example below:

Figure 10.1 Passenger Flow through a Bottleneck

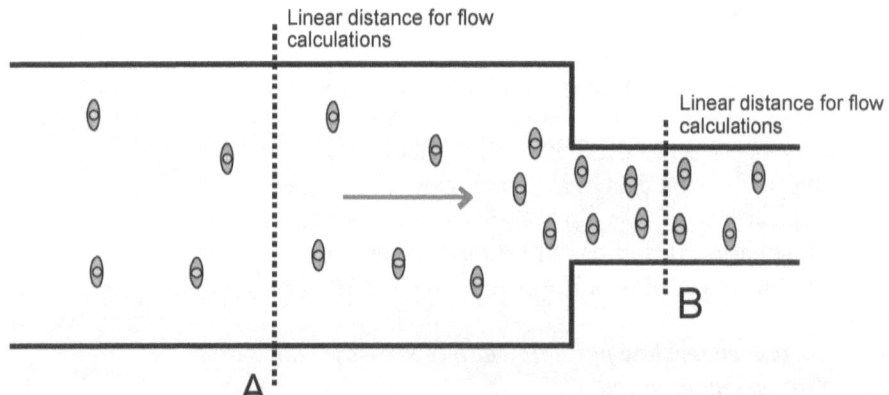

Passengers in the diagram above are moving from left to right. In the area with line A, passengers have plenty of room and can spread out, and so can move relatively quickly from left to right. Once they reach the area with line B, this more narrow area results in crowding, and so the average speed of passengers and their walking speed drops. The dashed lines represent the length used for the equations presented above. The length of the vertical line through A and B can be incorporated into the flow calculation, and passenger modelling packages commonly do this, quite effectively. Passenger flow modelling software packages can generate good results from this kind of analysis. The more passengers there are, the greater the effect of the bottleneck.

Station geometry is not always so clear and easy to calculate flow rates for. Where there are multiple corridors coming together into one area, with multiple entrances and exits, modelling of passenger movements is far more difficult.

Many studies have examined how quickly people walk, and this is needed to complete any flow calculations. As with anything involving people, there is a lot of variation, and some people move quickly and others are much slower. Numerous studies have looked at determining average speeds of movement, in a range of different scenarios. In practice two different sets of speeds are used for passengers in this situations; normal entry and exit from the station, and escape from the station under emergency conditions. Passengers will move much faster in an emergency situation.

Typical walking speeds for normal and emergency conditions are listed below. The speeds for emergency conditions are taken from the US standard NFPA130.

Walking Speeds Through Stations – A Rough Guide

Structure	Typical Speed	Comment
Normal Conditions		
Flat ground	45 - 75 metres/min	Depends on crowding, see below
Stairs, down	17 - 31 metres/min	Vertical direction
Stairs, up	12 - 21 metres/min	Vertical direction

Walking Speeds Through Stations – A Rough Guide

Structure	Typical Speed	Comment
Emergency conditions (from NFPA 130)		
Flat ground	61 metres per minute	Not linked to crowding
Stairs	15 metres per minute	This speed is upwards/vertical, not along the pitch angle
Barriers – fare collection	50 per minute	This flow rate is only used when barriers are de-activated
Turnstiles	25 per minute	

There is a lot of potential variation in the walking speeds listed above, as many people do not walk at average speeds. Also notice the large difference between the speed on flat ground and speed on stairs, with the stairs speed being much lower than flat ground.

Crowding is an important factor in walking speeds, with crowding reducing average speeds. People dislike and avoid touching each other, and in a crowd will attempt to avoid this. Where there is substantial crowding, people will walk more slowly as they attempt to avoid each other, and in cases of severe crowding, the movement of people may stop completely. As people move through areas restricted in size, they slow down and crowding increases. Areas of restricted size can form into bottlenecks where the crowding is sufficient to almost stop the movement of passengers through the station.

When performing these calculations, normally 0.5 metres from each wall is not included. Most people will not walk so close to the wall, and so this space is largely useless. So a corridor that is 6 metres wide has a useful width of 5 metres, with 0.5 metres being deducted from each side.

In the US the Highway Capacity Manual, which is for road vehicles using roads, prescribes 6 "levels of service" for describing the volume of traffic on a road. These LOS have been applied to station design, and used to describe the rate of movement of passengers through stations. These levels can be used to give an idea of the movement speed of passengers/people in a station. For completeness, the LOS categories are described below.

Passenger Flows – US system		
LOS	Space per pedestrian	Typical speed
A	>3.3 m^2 per person	79 metres/min
B	2.3 – 3.3 m^2 per person	76 metres/min
C	1.4 – 2.3 m^2 per person	73 metres/min
D	0.9 – 1.4 m^2 per person	69 metres/min
E	0.5 – 0.9 m^2 per person	46 metres/min
F	< 0.5 m^2 per person	<46 metres/min

This system is occasionally used outside of the US and Canada. London Underground uses this system as well.

The graph below shows the application of the above numbers to passenger flow rates per metre per minute. This is possible because there is both a speed and a density in the table above, which can be used to calculate the flow rate.

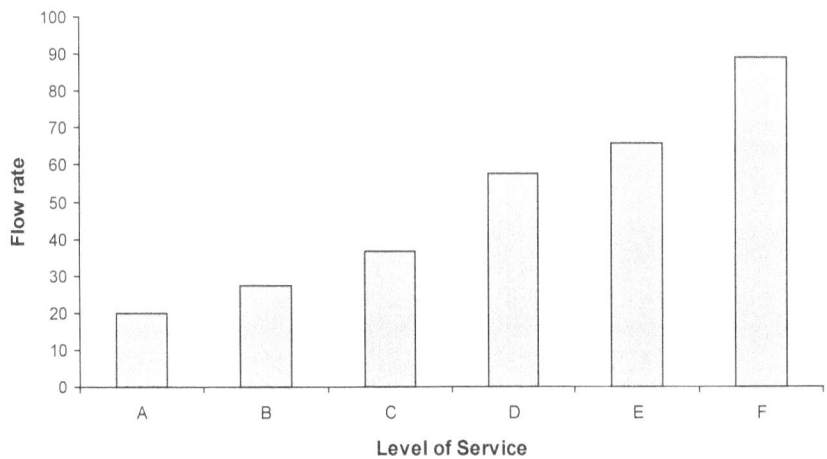

Passenger Flow (per metre per minute)

Notice that the flow rate increases as passengers become more crowded. At some point crowding becomes so great that the flow rate begins to decrease for any increase in crowding. It's not possible for the density of people to increase indefinitely, and an upper limit of about 100 people per metre per minute seems to be common, which can only be achieved at very high densities.

Some words about stairs; whilst on walkways people walk at constant speed and in no real pattern, on stairs people slow down as they climb, as they tire, and walk roughly one behind another. Stairs are often the major form of egress for underground and elevated stations, and so the rate at which passengers enter and leave is often strongly influenced by the size and number of stairs. Another consideration with stairs is that where passengers are moving in both directions on them, then the flow rate drops dramatically. Passengers ascend and descend at different rates, because climbing stairs is harder than descending.

Some simple definitions are needed for stairs. These are shown below.

Figure 10.2 Definitions for Stairs

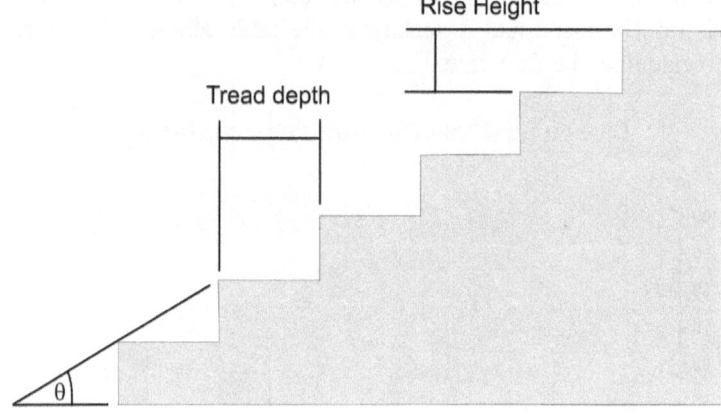

The simple diagram above shows some basic terms for stairs. Most countries have a building code or standard which prescribes the tread depth and the rise height. The pitch angle is commonly around 30°, but a range of pitch angles are common. It would be unusual for the rise height to be larger than the tread depth, which means most pitch angles are less than 45°. Steps in stations are no different from steps in any other facility.

For stairs three speed measurements are possible; in the vertical direction up and down, or along the stairs themselves. The third is the horizontal, and as most stairs are inclined less than 45° then this measurement will also be higher than the climbing speed, but lower then the speed along the stairs themselves. Where a number is provided for climbing or descending vertically, then this will be lower than any figures for the climbing speed measured at the same angle of the stairs.

Stairs for a station should be free of debris, clean, and even. Each step should be the same size, and even small changes in step height will result in a significant drop in speed for passengers either moving up or down the stairs. Stairs are also the same as walkways in the sense that overcrowding will result in a reduction in the speed of movement.

The size and shape of stairs will often be determined by any disability requirements in a country. Many countries have disability codes, legislation or regulations that describe how stairs should be designed. Station stairs will comply with national requirements on their design and geometry.

Station designers are confronted with a choice on the pitch angle of stairs; steeper stairs will require less space but will be more difficult to climb, and may not be suitable for the elderly and passengers with disabilities. In general stairs in a station should have a lower pitch angle, so that more people can climb them. There is however a penalty in the rate at which people will climb stairs. Shallower pitch angles also improve passenger comfort, as they are easier to climb.

One of the key dimensions for stairs, and then for any underground railway station, is the width of the stairs. As mentioned previously, most, if not all modern stations, are designed so that passengers can exit the platform, and then the station, in a small amount of time. In most cases the limiting factor in passengers leaving the station is the stairs, as they are limited in size and climbing stairs is in most cases slower then moving along flat ground. Another consideration is that most passengers, when confronted with a fire in an underground station, will attempt to exit the station through where they entered the station (assuming they entered the rail network through this station), as they know this path out of the station, and will attempt to use this route regardless of whether it is the most efficient and lowest distance to a safe place. This may mean that the number of people attempting to use a set of stairs in an emergency will be higher in one part of the station than another. This needs to be accommodated in any station design.

The wider a set of stairs, the more people that can use it. Flow rates for stairs are normally expressed in people per minute per metre. As an example of this calculation, consider the following example:

Flow rate = 50 people per minute per metre.

How many people would move through a staircase of 4 metres width in 90 seconds?

Total people = flow rate x time in minutes x width of staircase

So this is

Total people = 50 x 90/60 x 4 = 300 people.

Consider that the above example uses typical values, and this number of people being able to exit a station in this time may not be acceptable for a very busy metro station.

As the passenger density increases, the number of people moving up the stairs increases, until it reaches an optimum point. This density for stairs seems to be around 2.5 people per m^2, and after this point adding more people only slows down the rate at which they move through the staircase. Care must be exercised that in an emergency situation that this point is not reached when many people are fleeing to the stairs, as the movement of people will slow as more people want to exit and so a deadly situation may arise. At some point the movement of people through the staircase stops entirely, and the density is so high that no one moves at all. This point seems to be reached when the passenger density reaches around 5.8 people per m^2.

The graph below shows how the flow rate on stairs changes as the level of crowding changes. Notice that the flow rate seems to peak at about 2.5 people per square metre, or about 0.4 square metres per person. Recall that this was the highest passenger density used for flat open ground.

Passenger Flow Rates on Stairs

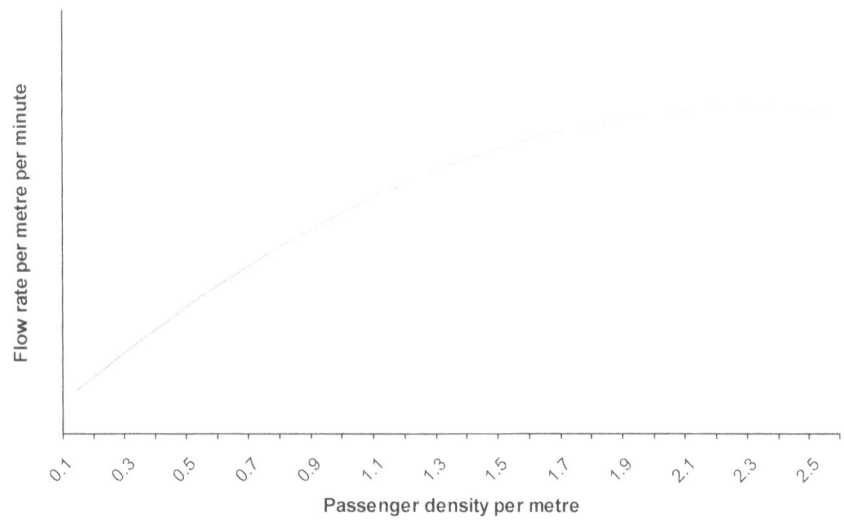

The flow rate on stairs is almost always lower than on flat ground, which again, makes the stairs the bottleneck in any station.

Little has been said so far about escalators, and large stations will normally have many. Escalators are normally installed in groups of two, but are sometimes installed on their own, and less common in groups of three. In even more rare cases, for very large stations, four or more escalators may be installed together. The rate at which passengers move along the escalator is determined by the depth of the step, and the speed at which the escalator moves. Escalators typically move between 0.5 to 0.75 m/s although higher speeds are common in rail systems in Asia.

Many escalators are designed so that two people may use them at the same time. The width of the escalator is such that two people can stand side by side in relatively comfort. Typically people on one side of the escalator walk up the escalator, and on the other stand for their journey on the escalator. The author's experience on escalators is that usually less than half the passengers on a train will wish to walk, and maybe 40% of the people alighting on from a train may wish to walk up or down an escalator.

Assuming both sides of the escalator are fully used, the formula for the flow rate of an escalator is:

$$Passenger\ flow\ rate\ (per\ minute) = \frac{1}{step\ size\ (metres)} \times escalator\ velocity \times 60$$

Smaller steps for the escalator improve the flow rate, but are more uncomfortable for customers.

A run-off is the area at the top or bottom of an escalator where passengers can alight from the escalator. This area is important for station design, as the lack of this area will result in passengers "bunching up" at the exit of the escalator. This can cause slower movement of passengers throughout the station. The size of the run-off needed is dependent on the flow rate through the escalator.

Passengers can have accidents on escalators where clothing or even limbs can get caught. In rare cases passengers may fall down them, which can cause substantial injury. An important rule in allowing passengers to use escalators is that they must wear sensible shoes, and not be barefoot. Some types of shoes, such as crocs, can get caught in between the step and the side of the escalator, so injuries will occur from time to time. It is also important for escalators to be fitted with an emergency stop.

Lifts, or elevators in the US, are very common in many different types of stations. Lifts are commonly installed to move passengers from the platform to the paid area near the barriers on the mezzanine level, and then from outside the unpaid area to the road or outside area. For an elevated station, there will normally be lifts to the area with the barriers, and then down to ground level.

Lifts are not installed to move large numbers of passengers. Typically lifts can move 12 – 16 people, although in many stations lifts are significantly smaller than this. In some rare cases large lifts are installed that can move 30 people or more, but this is quite uncommon. The slow movement speed of lifts means that its contribution to moving people out of stations is actually quite small. For the purposes of modelling passenger movements, it is acceptable not to include lifts at all, especially for calculations involving fire and life safety.

Lifts are very good for moving people who have disabilities, or otherwise have difficulty climbing up stairs. This actually includes a lot of different people:
- Those in wheelchairs
- The elderly
- The blind and those with vision impairment
- Passengers with lots of luggage
- Women with small babies, especially when they have strollers or prams for the baby
- Passengers in poor health
- Passengers who are obese or otherwise overweight
- Those who have difficulty climbing stairs
- Passengers who have become ill or otherwise had a medical emergency on the rail system

The provision of lifts in a rail system is a valuable service for customers. It is however a little expensive, and some rail systems avoid installing them because of the cost. Lifts should normally be installed in pairs, so that if one is out the other can be used. A large station may need several lifts, or even more, as passengers may need to move from different parts of the station down to the platform. Also note that lifts rarely connect the platform to an unpaid area outside the station, as many rail systems segregate their stations into paid and unpaid areas, and allowing passengers direct access to the station in this way may be considered a security risk. Some commuter rail stations have lifts where they connect directly from the street to the platform level, but again it is relatively rare.

Designing for Better Dwells at Stations

The headway of a rail line is the time between trains when the trains are travelling as quickly as permitted by the signalling system. For a stopping station one of the key parameters in determining the headway was the dwell time. The dwell time at stations is a component of the dwell time, and so the longer the dwell time, the larger the headway. Headway in many rail systems needs to be reduced as much as possible.

Station design is very important to the headway in very busy stations. Passengers need to be able to disembark quickly and efficiently without any obstructions. Obstructions, especially where the crowding is heavy, can have a pronounced effect on passenger speed. For the best possible passenger movement speed, it is important for passengers to have a pathway which is unimpeded.

The station below shows a typical situation in many metro stations. The train has stopped at the station, and is shown in light blue. People are disembarking from the train, but there is only one exit to the right of the station. Also note the small squares in brown, these are columns supporting the roof of the station, and old stations were often built with these kinds of structures. Columns are structural items that cannot be removed once installed without undermining the structural strength of the station.

Figure 10.3 Passenger Flow in a Poorly Designed Station

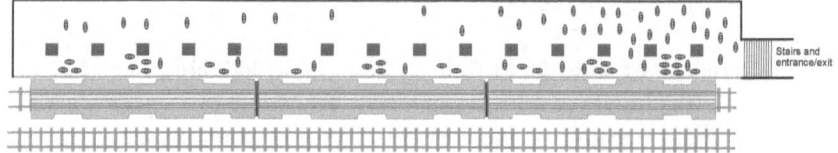

Also note in the above diagram that there is some congestion at the right end of the station, as passengers only have one exit. As passengers become more crowded they will slow down, and then they will slow down even more when climbing the only set of stairs into the station. This station is poorly designed.

In the station below many of the problems in the above diagram have been addressed. Notice that there are three exits rather than one, and these exits are located along the station. These exits can also be used as entrances. This station design will allow better loading and unloading of the train, and lower dwell times should passenger density get too high.

Figure 10.4 Passenger Flow in a Better Station

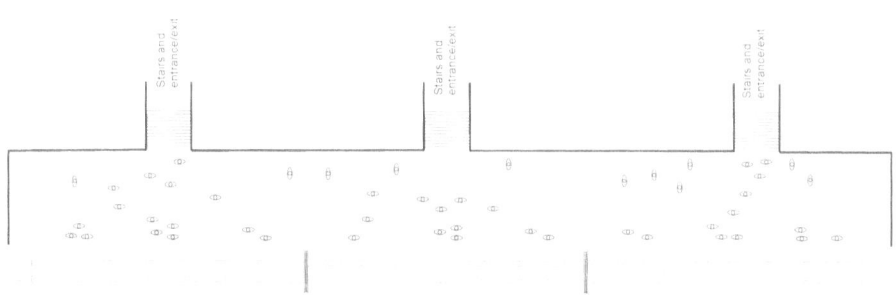

The station below shows as an example what can happen when construction costs are minimised to the point where the dwell time of trains arriving at the station is effected. One of the major costs of building an underground station is the cost of excavation, so minimising this cost through making the station smaller is one way to reduce costs. When taken to extremes, the size of the platforms can become very small, as in the diagram below. When side platforms are very small, passengers are crowded when alighting from the train onto the platform, and move very slowly when attempting to exit the station. The example below exists in some rail systems, and this kind of station can create major problems when passenger loads are high.

Figure 10.5 A Narrow Side Platform

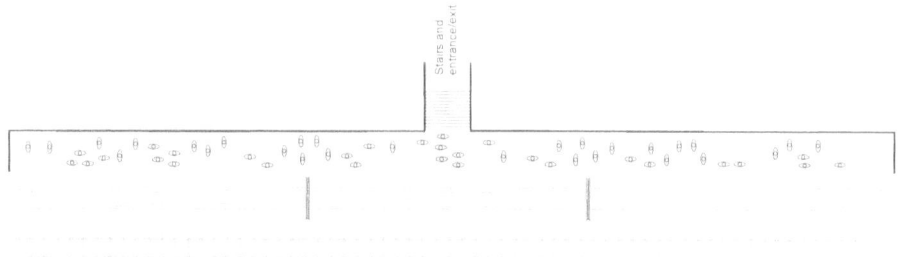

Platforms should be designed so that the highest anticipated passenger load will not result in excessive overcrowding. The ideal situation is that there should be at least 1 m^2 per waiting passenger at all times, although this may not always be possible. Where there is some special circumstance, or a special event nearby to a station, then in some cases it may be acceptable to allow for a more crowded station, and a space of 0.5 m^2 per waiting passenger may be acceptable.

Let's consider an example. Where a station is 160 metres long, and the peak passenger load is calculated to be 500 people per platform per minute. Assuming, a time between trains of three minutes, it would be necessary to allow for 1500 people standing along the platform. Without even allowing for passengers being closer to entrances and exits, and passengers alighting from the train, and surges in passengers entering the station, the platform would need to be almost 10 metres wide. With additional allowances, such as the space 0.5 metres next to walls which people rarely stand in, perhaps a platform width of 15 metres would be appropriate. This is quite large, and some platforms in metros are only 2 metres wide, far smaller than what is needed in many cases.

The example above demonstrates one of the advantages of an island platform. Island platforms almost always have two sides at which train can stop (although in rare cases three platforms are possible), with trains from each platform moving in opposite directions. Most stations have many more passengers travelling in one direction than another for many times in the day, so there will be large numbers of passengers moving in one direction, and a smaller number in another. Where this is the case, then island platforms will be able to accommodate more passengers as the other side of the platform can be used for waiting passengers. This idea is shown below.

Figure 10.6 A Narrow Side Platform

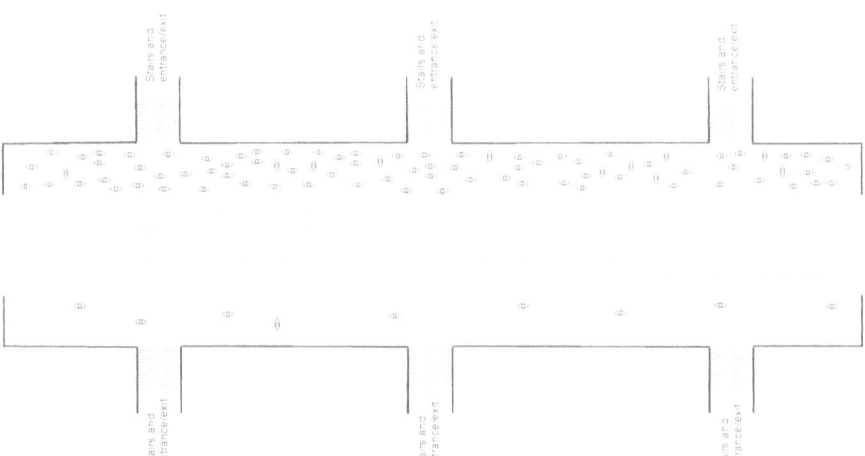

In the diagram above we can see that the top platform has a large number of passengers waiting for a train, and the bottom one only a small number. As a result the top platform is crowded, and the bottom one very comfortable. This scenario is very common in many metro stations.

Below is the same situation with island platforms, rather than side platforms. The same number of ovals representing people has been used in the diagram below as in other diagrams.

Figure 10.7 An Island Platform with the Same Number of People

For an island platform the platforms are in the centre of the tracks, and the platform has far more space for passengers to spread out. This configuration is much more desirable, as the larger platform area will allow passengers to move around more freely, and so be able to board and alight much more quickly from trains. Passengers alighting from the train can also make their way along the other side of the platform to the exits, which in this case are drawn at either end of the platform.

Crowding on trains is often very severe. Crowding on trains can be as high as 4 people per square metre, or in some very crowded systems up to 6 people per square metre. In India some rail services operate with supercrush loads, where 8 or even more people are standing per metre. This high level of crowding is acceptable on some rail services, but is generally undesirable. For platforms and station design it is even more undesirable, and should be avoided if at all possible. The level of crowding that is permitted on a train should always be higher than what is permitted on a station.

High levels of crowding will be particularly problematic where large numbers of passengers need to both board and alight from a train at the same station. Loading and unloading is dependent on the number of passengers boarding and alighting, and where almost all the passengers are boarding at one station, dwell times will be long. In many instances there are only a small number of large events in some cities, and so perhaps a high level of crowding is acceptable for these events. However, for most situations a high level of crowding is unacceptable, and should be avoided where possible. For stations which are near to venues with large crowds, larger platform areas may be needed to accommodate the large number of passengers.

In situations where passenger crowding on stations is extreme, then unusual problems start to occur. Passengers may not be able to get onto the train, and may need to wait for several trains before reaching the doors to board the train. Alternatively, for very busy services passengers may be overcarried, and not be able to alight at their desired station.

Passenger flow management is quite important, and can help in getting people to move faster. Passenger flows are much quicker when everyone moves in the same direction, and people entering and leaving the station do not cross each others paths. Consider the diagram below, we can see that passenger flows in stations can often cross each other. One common problem with passenger movements is that passenger flows are disrupted when they cross each other. In the diagram below, people are moving from top to bottom, and from left to right. Notice that in the middle the two flows intersect, and it is here that people slow down in their movement. Once through this blockage, people are free to move much faster.

Figure 10.8 Stations and Mixed Flows

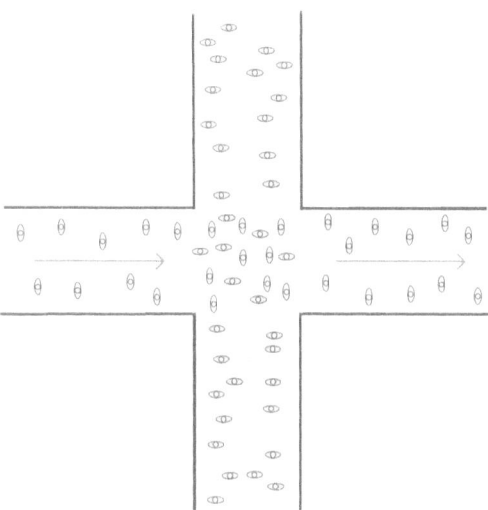

One of the goals of station design is to avoid the situation above. Once designed and built, it is difficult to manage passenger flows in stations, so that people moving in different directions do not block each other. Where possible, the above situation can be managed with separating out passenger movements, and this can often be done through lines and other markings on the floor of a station, or with lightweight barriers. These measures can be very effective in managing passenger flows.

The photo below shows one of the solutions to passenger flow in large stations, once they have been built. One way to improve passenger flow is to keep the flow of passengers in different directions separate, so that passengers can move faster. This can often be achieved by drawing lines on the floor of stations to indicate which way passengers should walk. Below is a photo where this has been done. Notice that the blue arrows indicate a direction up the stairs, and the yellow down the stairs. This keeps passengers moving in different directions apart, so that flow speeds can be maximised.

Stairs in a Station in Osaka

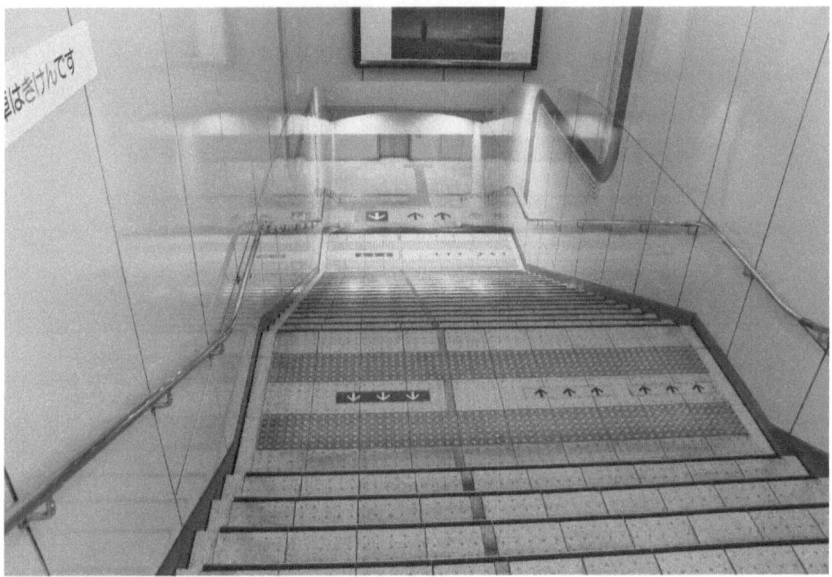

This photo was taken in Osaka in Japan. Notice that the space provided for passengers moving down the stairs is greater than moving up. This is because the platform is at the top of the stairs, and when passengers alight there is a large surge in passenger moving throughout the station, which is not the case for passengers entering the station, especially for stations that are not interchanges.

Chapter 11 Network Design around Stations

Introduction

The design of rail stations is not confined to the internals of the station. The design of the rail network in and around the station is just as important as the internal structure of the station. The rail network design in and around station defines how the station interacts with the rail network.

It is easy to assume that rail stations are always two platforms, with trains moving one direction from one platform, and the other direction from the other. In practise stations can come in a large variety of different configurations, with more or less than two platforms. Depending on the nearby junctions and other infrastructure, rail stations can terminate trains, or hold trains allowing other trains to pass them whilst sitting at the station platform. Stations can be used to organise and direct trains to different lines, and in some cases even divide and amalgamate trains. A variety of different operations are possible at a rail station, and many of these functions are very useful indeed.

There has been a trend away from more complex rail station designs, or at least this has been the trend in Australia. Certainly two platforms are simpler and easier to understand than deploying 1 or 3 platforms, and in the rail industry this has become the norm. The advantages of two platforms are clear, trains can move in opposite directions without being impeded, and it's a structure the public know and understand well. In general perhaps the principle is that where a rail system or line is being designed, the standard is two platforms, and where there is a case, then perhaps changes can be made.

Rail systems where more than 2 tracks are used for any more than a few hundred metres will often have stations with more than 2 platforms. It's not essential, but often there will be platform for each track where there is a station. In the Sydney rail system there are large numbers of this type of station, and trains can stop at the station on the track on which they are travelling. This chapter is not so much about this scenario, but about stations where additional tracks are added to provide operational flexibility.

Most rail systems are composed of long rail lines of two tracks. These rail lines can run for hundred of kilometres, with relatively little interruption. In Australia some two track rail lines run thousands of kilometres. In this scenario it is possible to install places where trains can be terminated, special stations where a train can stand and be terminated and sent in either of the two directions. This chapter is about this kind of station, where additional tracks and platforms are added to allow trains to be terminated. Another situation considered here is where a rail line divides (bifurcates) then more platforms and a more complex station structure may be needed to help manage trains.

Three or more platforms are typically used where trains are terminated, at the end of rail lines. Some rail systems have or had a policy of introducing terminus stations into a rail system at strategic points throughout, to allow rail lines to be divided into different operational zones should some kind of incident occur. Some rail systems in Australia contain significant numbers of 3 platform stations that perform this function. The author is a fan of so doing, and this operational flexibility can be very useful in the event of a large incident, be this a security incident or engineering failure. The case for this type of operational flexibility is clearer in long rail lines, such as over 30 kilometres, and definitely over 50 kms. The longer the rail line, the greater the need for this type of station.

How often larger stations should be installed into a rail system will depend on a variety of different factors. Where traffic is very low, there is no real need to install additional platforms as one train being terminated will not delay any others, as the service frequency is too low. Stations with additional platforms are normally installed where there is a reasonably high level of traffic, such as one train every 15 minutes or more frequent.

The design of any non-standard station will determine what additional functionality it will provide. Many different configurations are provided below, and their functionality varies depending on their design. The larger the layout, the more features that can be provided.

In many of the different station layouts below there are more than one platform where stations can move in one direction. This means that station information systems need to provide support to passengers to direct them to the appropriate platform. In the Sydney rail system, there have been numerous instances where passengers have been directed to the wrong train, and ended up in the wrong rail line in the wrong place. Where operational flexibility is introduced into a rail system then passenger information systems become much more important.

Detailed Drawing of Rail Systems

To show many different station types, and network designs, a convention has been adopted in this book for drawing tracks and platforms. These are outlined below, and platforms are in orange, and tracks in black. Arrows indicate possible train movement directions.

The drawing method below does not include signals. As almost all signalling schemes are very complex, the signals themselves have a lot of detail and information that sometimes can make the drawing a little difficult to read.

The level of detail show below is useful to show places where trains can be stabled, and can be turned back. Many of the common features of a rail system are shown. The running direction of the rail system is also shown. Stations and platforms are also shown.

So here are the basic elements of a rail system.

Basic Rail System Elements

————————	A rail track, with two rails, and sleepers in between. Only one train can move along this track at any one time.
◀	Possible direction of travel of a

Basic Rail System Elements

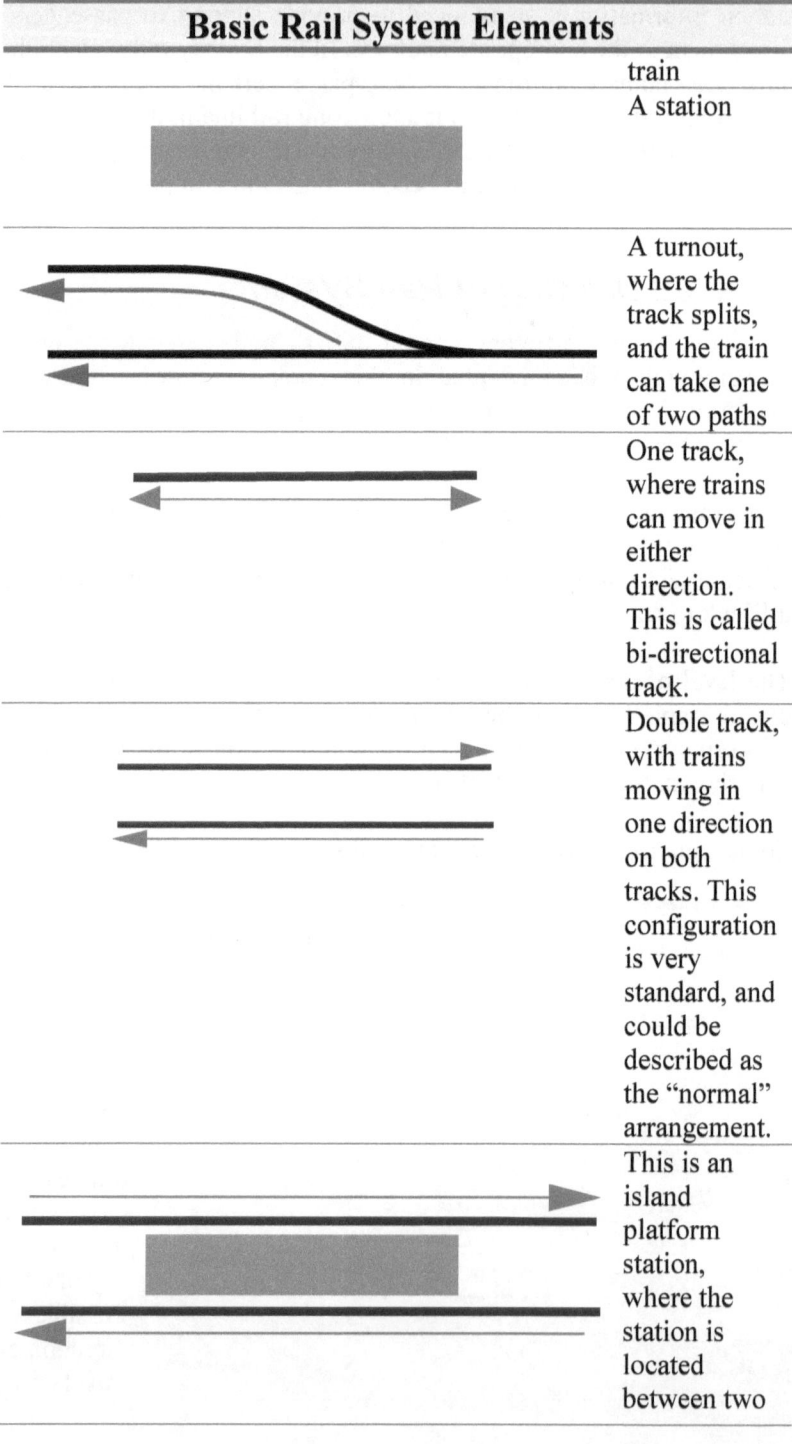

	train
	A station
	A turnout, where the track splits, and the train can take one of two paths
	One track, where trains can move in either direction. This is called bi-directional track.
	Double track, with trains moving in one direction on both tracks. This configuration is very standard, and could be described as the "normal" arrangement.
	This is an island platform station, where the station is located between two

Basic Rail System Elements

tracks. This is a very common configuration.

A station with side platforms. There is one station here, not two. Side platforms are sometimes used when space is limited or to save cost. Side platform stations are considered to have poorer customer service than island platform stations as for an island platform, staff can be placed in the middle of the station.

More complex arrangements can be built out of these basic elements. The table below shows how configurations can be built up into more complex structures.

More Complex Rail Layouts – Crossing movements

More Complex Rail Layouts – Crossing movements

	A crossover. Notice that part of the crossover is bi-directional, but most is not.
	A diamond crossover. Trains crossing over would need to wait until the any trains in the middle had passed before crossing over.
	A diamond crossing, or just simply a crossing. Trains cannot change direction here, but do pass over one track to continue on their journey.

From an infrastructure perspective, the addition of turnouts (especially in large numbers) can create a lot of additional work and expense, and additional turnouts should only be added when really needed.

Station Network Configurations

The design of the rail system in and around stations affects the way trains stop and arrive at those stations. Passenger trains typically terminate at stations, and not at other places in the network, as then passengers can be disembarked as far as possible into the train's movement to its final destination.

What is drawn below is a series of different configurations for stations that allows for a large degree of operational flexibility. The choice of what network design to choose depends on what is needed at that point in the network. Below are a series of different configurations that can be used.

The layout below allows for trains to be terminated on the middle road between platforms 1 & 2. Trains making their way along the bottom track can terminate on platform 2, and then move to the terminal road. Once there then the train can move in the opposite direction, normally once the driver has moved from one end of the train to the other. The train can then make its way to platform 1, where it can board passengers and move off to the right of the page.

Figure 11.1 Terminal Road

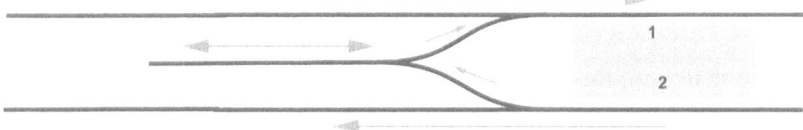

One of the advantages of the layout above is that trains can dwell in the terminating road waiting to be sent back. This feature can be very useful where there is a defect or failure in the train, and it needs to be moved out of the way from other trains.

In the layout below trains are terminated on platform 1. Trains can be terminated from either direction, but only onto platform 1. This will block trains moving from the left to the right, but trains can effectively change direction. This type of layout is inferior to a layout with 3 platforms, but is a common and effective way to get trains to be able to terminate.

Figure 11.2 Terminating in Both Directions

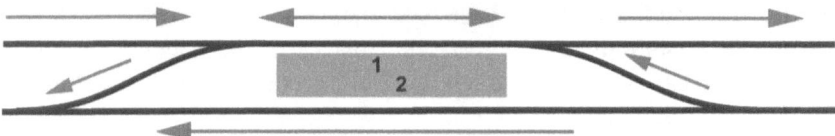

Notice that trains can also continue along from right to left, and stop at platform 1. Notice that it is not possible to terminate trains on platform 2.

The layout below there are three platforms, and two tracks turns into three at the station. Trains can be terminated on platform 1, and sent either to the left or right. This layout is very versatile and can provide a lot of operational flexibility for an operating railway. This type of layout is also useful for storing a slow moving train, which can be stored on platform 1. Platforms 2 and 3 are still useful for trains moving in their normal direction.

Figure 11.3 Terminating on No 1 Platform

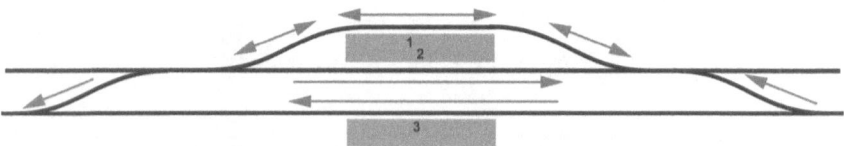

One problem with this layout is that it requires additional space. For an underground railway this additional space can cost money, and quite a lot at that.

The terminus below operates slightly differently than the one above. Notice that trains can terminate and stand on platform 2, and can wait there for a while whilst trains pass through platforms 1 and 3. The track next to platform 2 is sometimes known as a terminating road. This layout only allows trains to be terminated in one direction, from right to left. The advantage of this layout is there is no need for terminating trains to cross the path of any other trains, and so headway is not impacted.

Figure 11.4 Centre Terminating Road

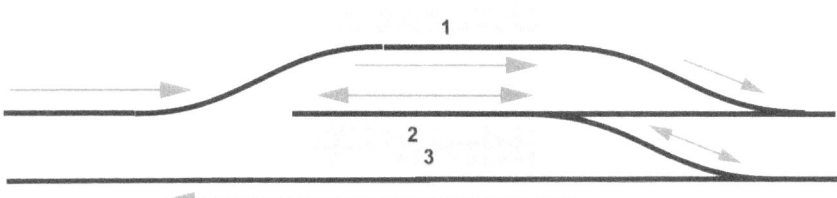

In the layout below trains terminate on platform 1. This layout is considered inferior to the other two above because trains need to cross in front of trains passing through platform 2 to get to platform 1. However, once there, trains can stand on this platform for some time until needed. Again, trains can only be terminated in one direction, from right to left, rather than from left to right.

Figure 11.5 Terminating Road away from Running Lines

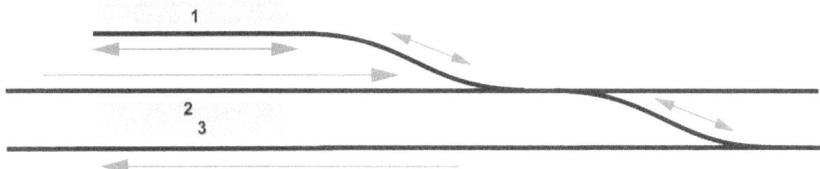

The layout below is a simple layout that minimises the use of space. Trains can be terminated on either platform, and then sent to the right. This structure of station is particularly useful for sending trains back to the right. One of the challenges of this layout is the use of a diamond crossover, which can require extra maintenance.

Figure 11.6 Terminating Station with a Diamond Crossover

The station layout below is a little more complicated than the ones above. In this layout there are 3 platforms and this is used to manage trains which are either making their way to or coming from the right hand side. There is a two track junction on the right, and trains are being managed at the station. Junctions such as the one below are common in many different types of rail systems, and adding operational flexibility to move trains around.

The layout below allows trains to be put from branch line (the one going up to the top), onto any platform. Trains sitting on platform 2 can also proceed to either direction. Trains sitting on platform 1 can also move either to the left or the right.

Figure 11.7 Platform Station with Junction

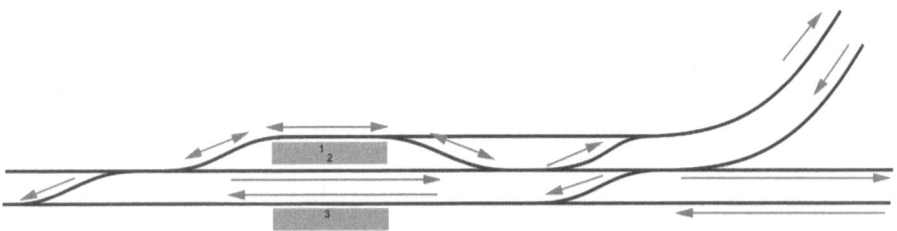

The layout below is for a terminus. A terminus is where a rail line ends and where many trains cease to be in revenue service. Terminus's are a very common feature of any rail system, and even metro systems have them. The layout below has 5 platforms, and is a common type of terminus.

Figure 11.8 Terminating Station

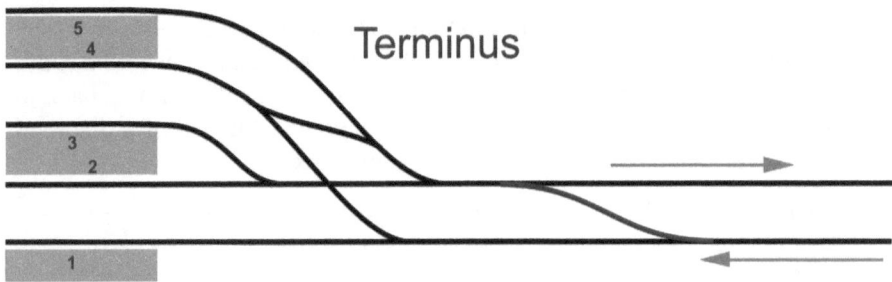

The layout below is a Barcelona style terminus. This means that trains that terminate at the terminus can open their doors on either side, and typically passengers disembark on one side and then embark on the other. Barcelona style stations are able to move large numbers of passengers quickly and efficiently.

Figure 11.9 Barcelona style Terminus

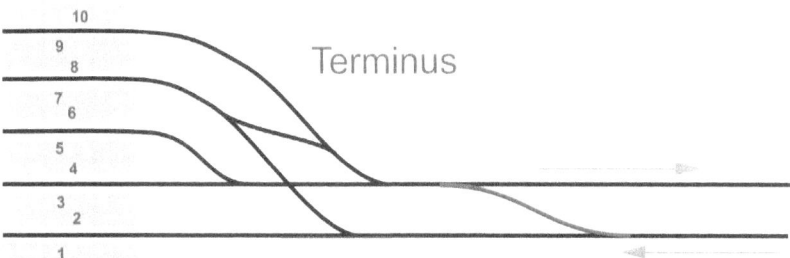

Chapter 12 Other Aspects of Station Design

Introduction

This chapter covers many of the miscellaneous features of rail stations. For example, stations consumer power, and this is discussed below. Also passenger movements into and out of stations is important, and this includes interchange stations, where passengers move from one rail line one to another.

Many different station configurations are drawn below. Also discussed in this chapter is the design of light rail stations, which is a special case for station design. There the relationship between road and rail design is the key, as light rail stations are often designed at the same grade as roads.

Exits and Entrances

Large stations can have very large numbers of people using it. This creates problems with getting people in and out of stations, as a single exit and entrance may not be enough for everyone to use the station.

For busy rail systems such as metros one important aspect of overall station design is the placement of entrances. Entrances should be placed in convenient places, which allow passengers to enter and exit the station efficiently. Poorly located entrances and exits can a string of problems, including:
- Longer journey times as passengers need more time to get to an exit
- Station crowding
- Poor passenger flows, and slow walking times
- Reduced utility of service, perhaps even affecting passenger numbers
- Large bottlenecks forming in stations

In short, placing exits correctly creates a better and more efficient rail system.

When we discuss entrances and exits it is important to note that in many cases an entrance serves as an exit as well. Entrances to many stations are sets of stairs, and passengers can move in either direction on these. Escalators move in only one direction, and so where there is only one escalator at an entrance or exit, the direction of the escalator will largely determine how the entrance or exit is used. This is especially the case where the escalator is moving in the down direction, and passenger need to walk up steps to exit the station, and they may not want to do this.

Where security is important, and everyone is checked before entering the rail system, then an entrance may require security equipment, and potentially not be usable as an exit. In China for example security scanning before entry to metro rail systems is common, so there may be entrances that are cannot be used as exits.

In practice more entrances and exits is better, especially for underground stations. Shinjuku station in Japan has over 200 entrances and exits, and there are entrances and exits scattered all around that suburb into the station. There is no real limitation on the number of entrances and exits, and more always seems to be better. Note that there are practical limits on the amount of vertical transportation that can be installed, escalators and lifts are expensive, consume lots of power, and need maintenance. It is common on large stations for only a small number of the entrances and exits to have vertical transportation, and the other exits are just stairs.

Below is a diagram of a very simple station design with two entrances and exits. They are located in the middle of the platform, and there is only one entrance/exit on either side. This cheap and efficient station design works well in many situations, and from a passenger perspective this design is very easy to understand.

Other Aspects of Station Design Page 201

Figure 12.1 Standard Station with Exits

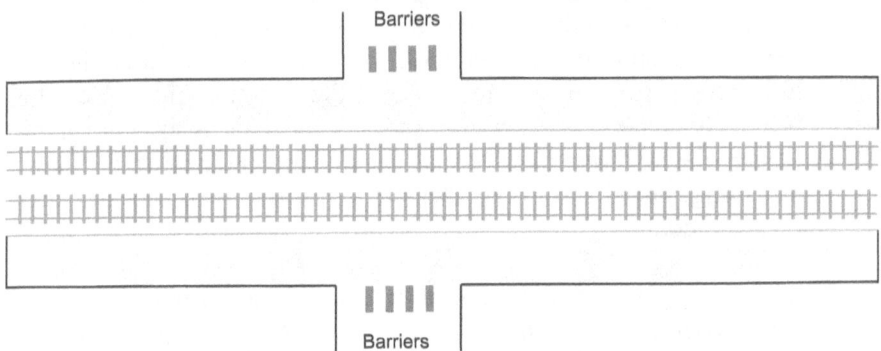

The station above shows a very common layout for station exits. There are two exits, one for either side of the station. The station is fenced, which is generally better to do, but not always done. Not drawn in 12.1 is the method for passengers to get from one side of the station to the other. There will be a way, and it may be something like a nearby bridge, a pedestrian subway, or even a pedestrian crossing. This station layout numbers in the several hundreds in Australia.

Commonly there would be parking on either side of this station, especially if it is a commuter station. A more elaborate station of this type would include a structure over the top of the station, to allow passengers to move from one side to another. This is shown below.

Figure 12.2 Standard Station with Exits through the Concourse

In this station the platforms are accessed through the concourse. Concourses can get very complicated, and in the next section much more complex ones are shown. The concourse is separated into two sections, with one side included in the paid area, and the other unpaid. Note that this station design allows for the public to use the station without paying, and cross from one side of the tracks to the other without entering the station paid area. This station design is superior and more complex than the simpler station design without the concourse.

Station entrances and exits will normally connect street level to the concourse.

Concourses

Concourses are large open areas where the barriers and entry to the paid area of the station is located. A concourse is where many of the facilities of a station are located, including toilets, passenger information, lifts, station staff, help points, ticketing, and potentially other facilities. Concourses come in three forms; above underground stations, above stations at ground level, and below elevated stations.

Concourses are very useful but their installation does increase the size of the station, and hence the cost. Concourses provide a place for

Other Aspects of Station Design Page 203

passengers to organise themselves and ask for information or use toilets. Shops may also be located on stations as well.

In an underground station concourses are places where passengers can be evacuated to. Platform level is one level below the concourse, and there can potentially be a fire there (or really a fire anywhere). One of the objectives for fire safety for an underground station is to evacuate passengers from the platform to the concourse as quickly as possible. Another objective is getting passengers from concourses out of the station as quickly as possible. The efficient design of the concourse, to get passengers in and out quickly, is important.

The drawing below shows a typical concourse. It has 4 exists, a paid area, and stairs connecting to the platform in the middle of the paid area. This type of concourse is "standard" and represents a reasonable level of design, and has many of the features that are attractive for a concourse.

Figure 12.3 Light Rail Station on the Side of the Street

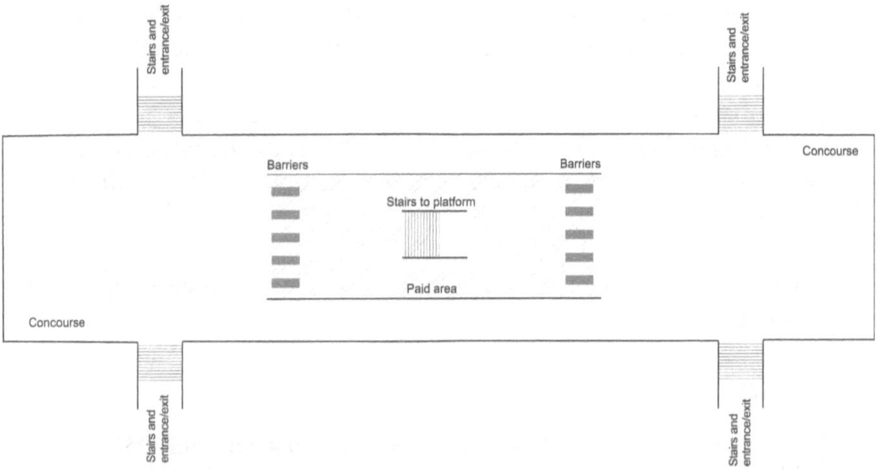

We note the above concourse has the following advantages:
- There are two sets of barriers, which allows flexibility in how they are configured to allow passengers into and out of the paid area
- There are two connections between the left hand side of the concourse and the right hand side

Other Aspects of Station Design Page 204

- There are 4 exits from the concourse to the outside, and these can be either down or up to street level.
- The concourse is large and provides ample space for passengers

So now below is an inferior design for a concourse.

Figure 12.4 Low Quality Concourse Design

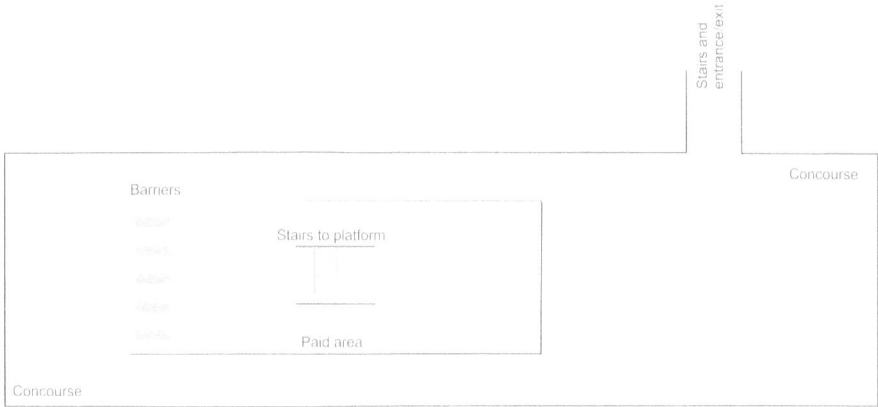

This concourse design is substantially inferior to the one above. There is only one exit, and the barriers face the opposite side of the concourse and not towards the exit. This station will have many problems with passenger flow, as passengers need to move from the stairs to the barriers and vice versa. Passenger flow will be messy and slow. Another problem is that the exit to and from street level may be extremely busy, as there is no alternative pathway. The number of problems with this kind of station abound, and the reader may think that this station design is impossible, but there are stations designed this way. Even some bush stations have this design.

The diagram below show a common mistake with station design. The paid area fills the entire space from top to bottom, so there is no way for passengers to get from one side to another without entering the paid area. The problem here is that passengers may exit the paid area on the left, and want to exit on the right. As they are now through the barriers, normally they cannot pass through again and so will need to exit the station through the exit they don't really want.

Other Aspects of Station Design Page 205

Figure 12.5 Large Paid Area

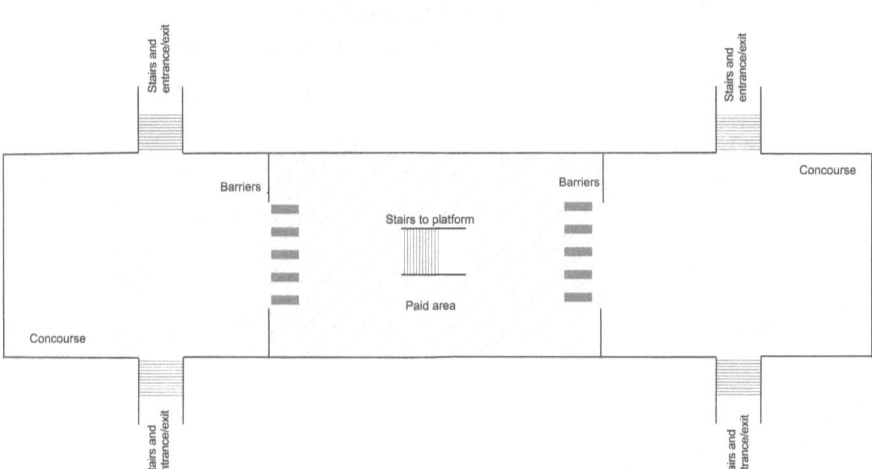

It is generally better if passengers exit from stations as close to their intended destination as possible. This reduces the time taken for the trip, and also the number of road crossings pedestrians needs to make. Where a station is busy, and passengers need to cross streets, these street crossings can become very busy, which through effective station design may have been completed unnecessary.

Stations are often underground and built under roads, Where this happens then is it best if there are multiple exits. The problem of course is cost, and constructing large concourses can make things very expensive. It's easy to say to build a large high quality concourse, but sometimes the budget simply isn't there.

Where trains are very long, such as commuter trains, what is sometimes done is to construct stations with two separate concourses. The author has seen designs proposed for stations with three separate concourses. Below is a diagram showing what this rather unusual situation would look like:

Other Aspects of Station Design Page 206

Figure 12.6 Split Concourses

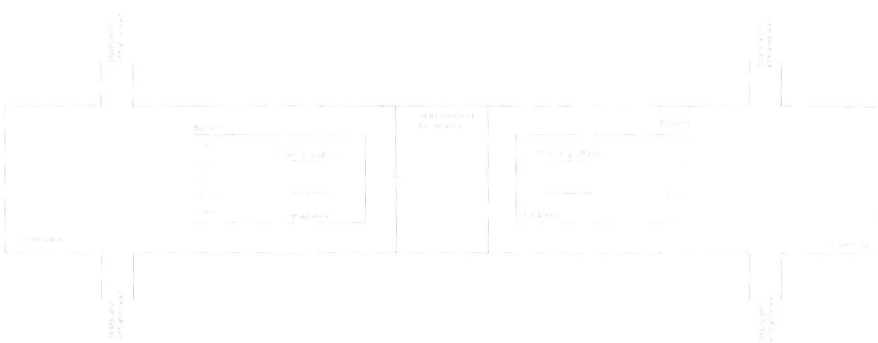

A number of stations exist in Australia with this structure. There are two concourses, and all the exits are located far away from each other. The exits from one side of the station can only be reached through the paid area, and the platform, which is a difficult path and not an attractive option. There is no access for passengers through the station back of house areas.

For a station designed as above things can be very confusing for passengers. There are two stairs connecting the station to the concourse, and depending on which they take then the choice of exits is limited.

Overall this structure of station has a number of issues which mean that it should be avoided where possible.

Figure 12.7 Station Infrastructure

The diagram above shows the situation when station infrastructure is located in the centre of a concourse. This unusual situation should be avoided where possible, and infrastructure should be separated from public areas as much as possible. This is particularly the case for power, such as high and low voltage, or traction power. Electrical assets can catch fire, and whilst this is unusual, a substation fire occurs per substation perhaps every 500 years (as an average). Where many substations are located in station, this can become a real problem. This problem is especially serious where infrastructure is located near the only means of egress from the station, which is how the station above is constructed.

Interchange Stations

Interchange stations are places where multiple rail lines are connected through the rail station, and passengers must alight to get to other rail lines. Passengers are able to move from one line to another and board another train. Whilst many interchanges are designed well, many are not, and rail system designers face many challenges with interchange stations.

One important parameter in the design of interchange stations is the time taken for passengers to get from one set of platforms to another. The best interchange stations are constructed so that one set of platforms sits above the other, and the interchange time is almost nothing, perhaps 20 or 30 seconds. Other interchange stations are very large, and the connection between different sets of platforms may take several minutes, or in unfortunate cases even longer than that. Overall rail travel times can be badly affected when the travel times becomes very long, and so correctly designing the interchange is very important.

The most common scenario for an interchange is where there are two sets of tracks, for a total of four tracks. There are two platforms, each with two tracks, and there is connection between the two platforms. Whilst the author has not taken a poll of how many different types there are, this would be the majority of interchange stations. In rare cases there are three rail lines coming together, but typically there are two.

Interchange stations can be described through how the different sets of platforms are connected. Passengers need to walk from one platform to another, and different connection possibilities are:
- From one platform to another directly
- From the paid area (but not the platforms) to one another
- From each concourse
- Through public streets or shopping centres

The above list is in order of best to worst, and where interchange is through public streets the interchange station is not very effective. There are many of this type of interchange station.

The distance between the different sets of platforms will normally determine how to connect the two together. Connections from one platform to another requires the platforms to be extremely close together, and this can be done through a large terminus station. Paid areas are normally relatively small, so sets of platforms to be connected in an interchange station would need to be within 100 metres of each other, typically, to connect through the paid area. Where connections are several hundred metres, or even over a kilometre, then at best connections are through concourses.

Some of the more common problems with interchange stations are:
- Two or more rail lines are far apart, and their interchange stations are far apart, and passengers need to walk large distance to get from one to another
- Poor signage means that it is not clear what direction to go to get to the other rail line
- Numerous flights of stair connect different rail lines together, which is a challenge for many passengers to negotiate
- Problems with ticketing, where tickets may not work from one line to another, or passengers need to go out of the paid area to reach the other rail line and do not realise they need to do so
- Some interchange stations are extremely large, and can be difficult to get around due to their size (such as Shinjuku station in Tokyo)
- Walkways between rail lines are little more than construction sites, with poor footing, broken surfaces, barriers around construction work, and poor signage.

- In some cases there may be multiple stations to interchange with, and signage needs to identify which is the correct one for passengers to walk to, and to get to their final destination.

The ideal construction of interchange stations should allow passengers to easily and quickly move from one rail line to another. Ideally, interchange stations should have platforms close together, so that the interchange time is small. Good station design will allow passengers to interchange without going to far, and in Hong Kong it is possible to interchange between rail lines by moving from one side of an island platform to another. This is done by designing stations so that trains arrive on two sides of a platform moving in the same direction.

The photo below shows a moving walk. A moving walk is similar to an escalator, but along flat ground. Moving walks do not have stairs, and are there to assist passengers in getting quickly from one place to another. Moving walks are common in airports, and also in large interchange stations. There are a number of large moving walks installed in stations in Hong Kong at interchange stations. The moving walk shown below is located at the Domestic Airport station in Sydney, where it is used to connect the two terminals together though the underground station.

A Moving Walk

Figure 12.8 An Interchange station – connected through the concourse

The station above is an interchange station which is connected through the concourse. The paid areas for the two connected stations are not connected. This structure of station is very common, and is really two separate stations connected through a pedestrian walkway. The way this station is drawn suggests that the station is underground, although it is possible to structure a station this way above ground as well. Note the moving walks connecting the two stations, making them one larger station.

On the rail system map this station may be identified as one station, or as two. This may depend on the distance between what are really two separate stations, although common practice seems to identify these stations as one station.

The station below is connected through the paid area.

Other Aspects of Station Design Page 211

Figure 12.9 An Interchange station – connected through the paid area

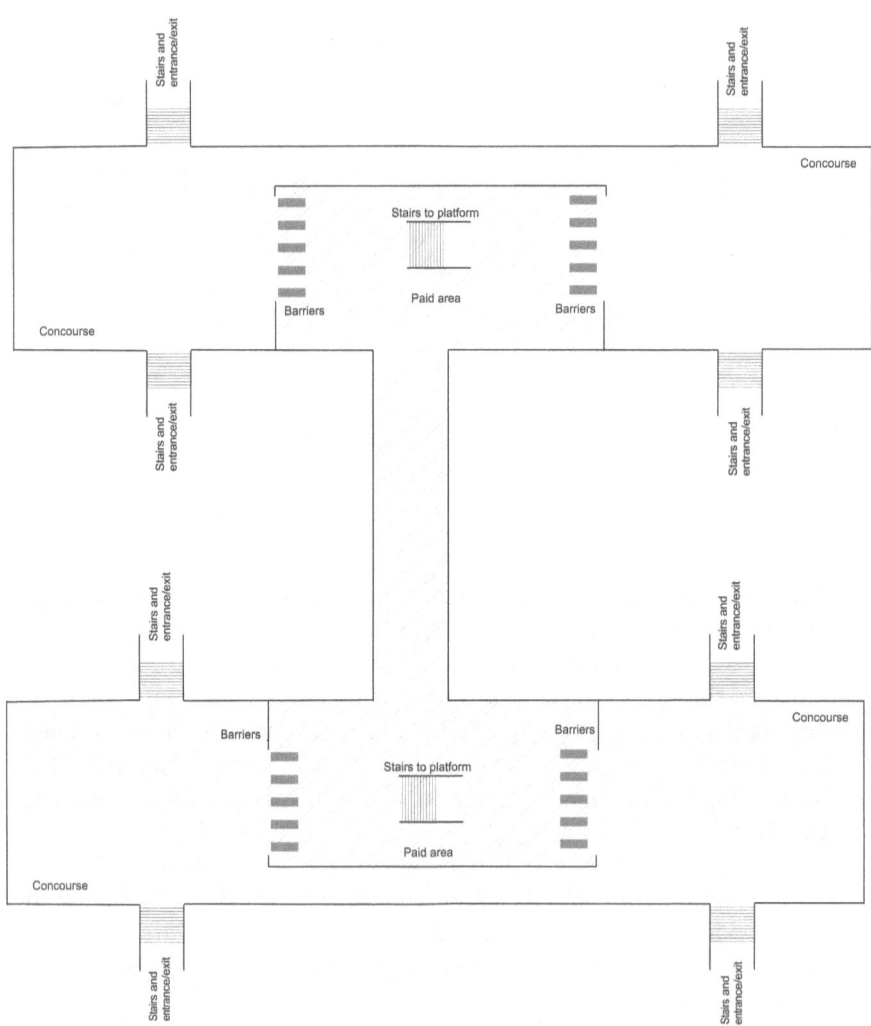

Short Platforms

In some cases the length of the platform may be shorter than trains which use the platform. Whilst this situation may seem a little silly, in some railways it is common, and passengers can only disembark from parts of the train there is a matching platform next to the door. Where there is no platform next to the train, people wanting to disembark may decide to leap from the train onto the ground below.

Where a train stops at a station that is shorter than the train, its best if the train is configured so that the doors with no matching platform don't open. This requires rollingstock of a special type, and programming to direct the doors not to open. It's better to have this technology if at all possible, but at the time of writing this book in Sydney there are still dozens of stations where the platform is too short, and no technology to stop all the doors from opening, although something is planned in this area. So it is possible for this situation to exist, even in modern times.

Regional trains can be very long because passengers need to sit down, making the passenger density rather low. In some cases platforms where the train stops are not long enough, so doors will face nothing but grass or open space. Furthermore the drop down from the train door may be quite large, and so any passengers that attempt to alight down to the ground are risking injury. In rare cases most of the train may have no matching platform, and disembarkation may be impossible from several carriages of the train.

For obvious reasons it is far better if all platforms are as long as the train itself. In a metro or any other system that operates in an urban environment, this will generally be the case. In some rail systems that operate to remote places, where the number of passengers per day can be counted in the dozens, building a full station may not be appropriate. Alternatively, and this sometimes happens where the station is located next to a river or other body of water, it may not be possible to build a station to the length needed as space is severely constrained, and so a compromise is made. In many cases the local residents may be prepared to accept a reduced length platform as long as there is some sort of rail service.

For any railway that creates this situation there are a number of factors that need to be considered:
- Where passengers jump from the train and are injured, how will medical assistance be provided?
- What happens where a passenger does not know that their carriage does not have a matching platform, and cannot alight, and so are overcarried to the next station. Will a taxi be provided? Overnight accommodation? What happens if

children are overcarried, is the railway going to allow them to find their own way home if they are overcarried at night?
- Which doors on the train are to be opened? Will it be the front doors or the back ones? Someone in the middle perhaps?
- How can passengers be informed that trains cannot provide exit to certain stations? Perhaps posters on station walls, or announcements to passengers.

Overall if at all possible stations should be constructed to at least the same length as the longest train, but in a small number of cases it may not be appropriate to do this.

Cover for Passengers from the Elements

Underground and elevated stations in major rail systems are almost always protected from the rain. There is complete coverage of the railway station, and heavy rain will not effect the movement of passengers and trains. In regional or commuter systems, almost all stations will be above ground and be exposed to the elements. The station below is common in some rail systems and the covered area is very small. This station is in Perth in Australia, and like many stations in that city has almost no coverage of the platform.

An Uncovered Station

For small stations there is no real reason why the entire platform should be covered. During rainstorms passengers can wait under the small shelter provided, and this will be adequate in most cases. For larger stations, lack of coverage can be a problem, as passengers will want to avoid getting wet, and will all wait under whatever cover is provided. Where the covered area is small, it will be come very crowded, and when boarding any trains there will be delays are the passengers will all crowd into one or two doors. This can create serious problems with dwell time, as passengers will attempt to board trains only through train doors next to covered areas.

Stations that are only partly covered will need less cleaning, as rainwater will wash away any dirt, especially where the station is designed with a slight slope on the platforms to allow rainwater to run away. Sunlight can sterilize the floor of any platform, in time, so this means that sanitising agents may not be needed to clean the platform. As a general rule, stations should only be covered if needed, and there is nothing wrong with leaving a station partly uncovered.

Straight and Curved Platforms

Many station platforms in large metro systems are straight, and when trains arrive they will sit in a straight line from one end of the train to another. Many platforms are curved, and not straight, and this is common in large commuter rail systems. In Australia many stations are curved, some dramatically so, as building straight stations was not considered to be important until relatively recently.

A curved platform is shown below. This station is in Hong Kong, and has side platforms. Notice that the platform on the left is concave, and on the other side of the two rail tracks, convex.

A Curved Platform in Hong Kong

The problem with curved platforms is demonstrated in the diagram below. Train carriages are built straight in all cases, and can only bend or articulate where there is a coupling between carriages. Light rail vehicles can be articulated, which means that there can be a number of joins, which allows the vehicle to appear to be curved, but in reality is made up of many short straight sections. Commuter and regional trains especially can have very long carriages, 26 to 30 metres in length is common, and passenger doors will often be located at each end of the carriage. Placing a straight object alongside a curved one will mean that in some places the carriage will be close to the platform edge, and in others far away. In extreme cases the door/carriage floor may be over 30 cm away from the platform, and with such a large gap passengers can fall into it. This may cause injuries, or even death.

The diagram below shows the problem. The centre of the carriage is close to the platform edge, and any doors located there will not have a large gap. Doors close to the end of the carriage, and they are commonly located there on double decker carriages (bi-level), will be further away from the platform.

Figure 12.10 Platform Gaps

This situation is considered extremely undesirable. Passenger with disabilities, for example those with vision impairment, will struggle to contend with such a large gap, and may fall through. Passengers with wheel chairs will need some sort of mechanical assistance to cover such a large gap, and will not be able to cross this without help. Where gaps of this size exist, stations will need to be manned, and staff provided to allow wheel chair passengers to board the train. Typically a ramp is provided to wheelchair passengers to allow them to cross this gap.

Consider that where this assistance is not provided, and many regional and commuter trains are not staffed throughout the entire day, then wheelchair passengers may not be able to board a train at all. Alternatively, wheelchair passengers may not be able to alight, and may be overcarried to the next station that is staffed or where the platform and the floor of the train are close enough that the passenger can alight without assistance. Also consider that mothers with prams may also struggle to get onto and off trains. There are a large number of different passengers who are disadvantaged by this station design.

Having said all this, there are some situations where a curved platform is unavoidable. Metro stations and stations will high volumes of passengers should always be designed so that they are straight, and this is a common requirement in the standards for passenger design. However, some very small stations may only have a very small number of passengers, and it may be acceptable for a rail line and corresponding platform to be curved. Consider that there may be laws and regulations that prohibit this in many countries, as this station cannot be used by those with disabilities, even when the number of passengers using the station is very small. This is the case in Australia, and in all future construction all platforms are straight.

Note that curved platforms can be both convex and concave. In diagram 12.10 the platform shown is concave, and this is more common, as island platforms often contain a station building or other facilities in the middle, making the centre of the station wider than the ends. Concave platforms are much more common than convex, as many island platforms have two concave platforms.

So the reader has seen the need to have straight platforms, and the benefits this brings. Building rail lines with straight platforms raises many challenges also, and these include:
- Straight stations are a lot easier to achieve geometrically with side platforms rather than island platforms. Side platforms are not as suited for large passenger flows as island platforms.
- Island platforms, combined with straight platforms, will mean that the rail tunnels leading into a station may need to be twin bore, rather than single bore. A single bore tunnel may be impossible as it would be too large, so two tunnels are needed rather than one. This substantially adds to the construction cost
- Curves along any rail system with straight platforms will need to be sharper, as no curves are permitted along platforms, and curves in most rail systems are very common. In some cases the curves may need to be so sharp that maximum speeds need to be reduced, and so average travel speeds are reduced.
- In severe cases, especially where rail lines are following some geographical feature such as a river or a harbour, it may be impossible to construct entire stations, as the geometry does not permit the construction of a station without curves.

Straight platforms can be difficult to implement, and present a very serious challenge to rail designer. Clever design, and well thought out transport plans, can go a long way to manage this problem.

Reusing Disused Stations

Many older rail systems were installed during the 19th century, and were very large. Rail transportation was the dominant mode of transportation use for decades, especially in the early 20th century, so rail systems in many countries were very extensive. As cars and trucks became more common many railways around the world, and this was particularly the case in Australia, shrank or were closed. This resulted in many old stations falling into ruin or being closed. In Australia there are dozens of this kind of station.

Below is a photo of an old disused station in the Central Coast in NSW in Australia. Note that the rail lines are covered with grass, but the tracks are still visible. The people at the platform are from the local historical society, who volunteer their time to maintain the station, mow the grass, pick up any rubbish and sweep the floor.

Disused Station

Old disused stations offer some opportunities for rail designers, as they can sometimes be refurbished and put back into service. Often the space and land is available for rail services, because the station was obviously previously used for trains, so this is easy. Also some buildings can be reused, but often new ones are required. Sometimes, and it is fortunate when this happens, that when the station was closed there was no need for it, and after decades, and so the station can be returned to service.

Some of the problems with returning old stations to service can be:
- No one wants to use the station, as this is why it was closed in the first place
- The structure is too weak to support modern heavy trains, especially if there are any bridges in and around the station
- Services, such as electricity and water, are non-existent
- Land has been sold that would allow the use of the station

The most famous case of a refurbished station is St Pancreas station in London. Opened in 1868, it was bombed during World War 2, and by the sixties was run down and in poor condition. Several attempts were made to demolish it, but it was saved, particularly by the efforts of John Betjeman. By the early 90's a handful of services were using the station consistently each day. It was refurbished for use as the terminus for High Speed 1, the rail link that passes under the English channel to France from London. The refurbishment was extremely expensive, costing over 1 billion US dollars. Now the station is considered an architectural marvel.

Light Rail Station Design

One of the advantages of light rail and tram systems is that they can be designed with little separation between the rail system and road vehicles and often operate at the same grade. This reduces the cost of construction, and makes them very accessible to public transport users, as they are at street level and usually not buried deep underground. In many cases these systems have no separate right of way. Trams often operate down the middle of roads, and in many ways are treated the same as any other road vehicle.

As light rail and trams are located in and around roads, the question arises as to the placement of track and rail corridors in comparison to where roads are located. The right of way for rail may or may not be separate from road vehicles, and a large number of different configurations are possible, and some of these are shown below:

The figure below shows a rail corridor in the middle of a street, with road vehicles on either side. This is a common design for light rail stations, and the use of a separate right of way for rail track is a good idea. For this design passengers will need to cross the road on one side or the other of the station to exit the corridor. Passengers will also need to cross the tracks to get to the other light rail station to go in the opposite direction to the one in which they came.

Figure 12.11 Light Rail Station in the Middle of the Street

Below is another configuration for a light rail station, and the light rail station is on the left. The road is separate from the light rail station, although alongside one another. The light rail station is an island platform, so passengers will need to cross one track to get to the side of the road. This configuration is a very good one, as road and rail traffic is separated.

Figure 12.12 Light Rail Station on the Side of the Street

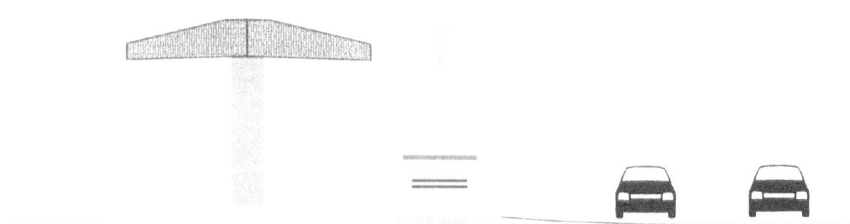

The light rail configuration below is extremely common in tram systems, but is also used in light rail systems as well. Road vehicles and rail share the same right of way, and mix freely. Whilst road vehicles can overtake trams, the converse is not true. This structure can work quite well, and is common in Melbourne with the large tram network there. One of the drawbacks with this structure is that passengers who wish to board and alight onto the tram must cross roads with fast moving vehicles on it, and the potential for an accident is quite significant. This configuration, whilst cheap and easy to implement, is not the safest, and is generally not recommended unless it cannot be avoided. There are however, many instances in a large tram network where there is no alternative, and this configuration is suitable.

Figure 12.13 Mixed Light Rail and Road Traffic with some Separation

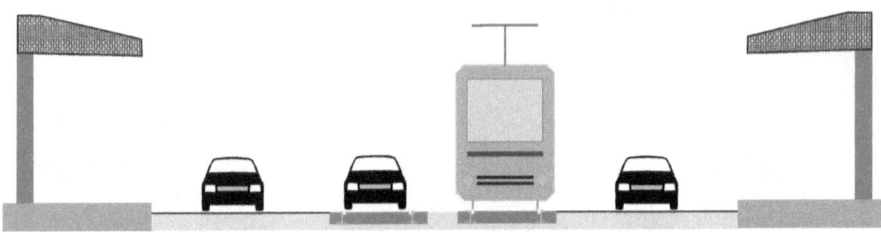

Also notice with the above configuration that road vehicles drive on the steel rails that support the light rail vehicle. Where the width of the road vehicle and rails are the same, it is possible for the road vehicle to slide along the rails, and not be able to stop when needed. This is particularly a problem in the wet, and accidents can be quite common.

The light rail configuration below is a poor one, but also somewhat common, especially in Melbourne. There is no separate right of way for rail traffic, and so road vehicles and trams/light rail share the same space. There is no way for road vehicles to pass the rail traffic, which is likely to be slow. As trams/light rail stop to allow passengers to board and alight, these vehicles will stop and wait at the tram stop. As the rail vehicle waits at the stop, road vehicles need to wait also. For a very busy street, passing through a congested shopping area, the travel speed of the tram/light rail vehicle may be very slow, to the point where there is no point in providing the service at all.

Figure 12.14 Mixed Light Rail and Road Traffic

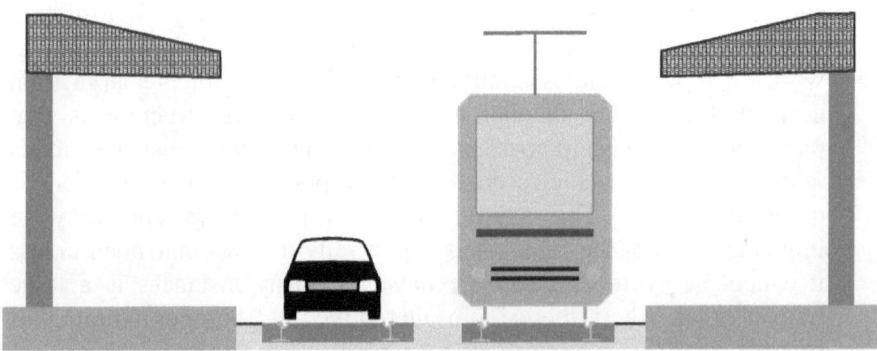

Tram systems were once very common in many parts of the world, especially Europe and North America. Almost all of them have been removed, and only a small number exist in their old form. One of the major contributing reasons for this was the use of the configuration above, which blocked road traffic and greatly contributed to congestion. The survival of the Melbourne tram network, now the world's largest, was because the configuration used above was rarely used, and so problems with congestion were avoided. The configuration above should only be used when absolutely necessary, and when there is no alternative.

Managing Power Consumption and Station Environmental Management

Power Consumed in Stations and other Facilities

Power consumption is something that should be considered in the design of any station. Whilst it might seem to the reader that design choices are limited, the reality is that there is much that can be done to reduce power consumption in a station. This is especially so for underground stations, or those that are covered and require artificial lighting.

Stations consume a lot of power. Stations may consume over 50% of all the power consumed by a rail system. Many of the systems installed in stations can consume a lot of power. Some of the typical systems and facilities that consume all this power include:
- Shops, especially those that cook or provide food
- Advertising displays
- Lighting
- Wireless internet
- Lifts and escalators
- Facilities for stations staff
- Air conditioning
- Platform screen doors

Larger stations consume more power than smaller ones. Reducing the size of a station is one way to reduce power consumption, and the power consumption per square metre of public area can be constant across many different station types, so smaller stations consume less power than large ones. A modern trend has been to increase the size

Other Aspects of Station Design Page 223

and space of stations, as this give a feeling of space and luxury, and many large terminus stations have been designed this way. One should remember however that larger stations, with a greater floor area and volume, will need more power to be air conditioned and lit.

Deeper underground stations will consume more power. As mentioned above, it is generally recommended for any station built underground to be as close to the surface as possible, as this makes evacuation easier in the event of a fire or any other emergency. Deep stations require more power to move people from the platform to the surface, and the deeper this is the more power that is consumed. Where the station is particularly deep, multiple escalators may be needed, as one escalator will be either too short to reach from the platform to the surface, or the capacity may not be enough, or that there is no room to fit the escalator in. Multiple escalators will consume more power than one on its own.

Lifts and escalators have been substantially redesigned in recent years to reduce their level of power consumption. Escalators have been designed that operate only when passengers are detected moving onto it (or standing on it), so escalators operate only very slowly when no one is using it. This can save a lot of power.

The power consumed in stations, workshops, shops and cleaning equipment, can be a significant percentage of the power consumption for a railway. Certainly in Sydney the power consumed at stations is relatively low, as the pleasant and comfortable weather means that air conditioning at stations is rarely needed, something that consumes a lot of power. In Singapore on the other hand on some lines the power consumed in stations is greater than the power used for moving trains, and this is probably because of the need to air condition stations in that country. It is possible to achieve reductions in power consumption in stations, and below are some fairly standard measures that can be implemented in stations to reduce the power consumption:

- Platform screen doors retain the air conditioned air within the station. The are particularly effective in cities where the temperature is either very hold or cold
- Special lighting systems can reduce the power needed for lighting by about 30%. There are a number of different technologies, including voltage regulation and special types of fluorescent tubes
- Reducing the number of entrances and exits into the station

- Installing escalators that slow down when no one is using them. These escalators can detect when passengers step onto them
- Special types of lifts consume less power moving people up and down
- Overall the energy consumption of a station is usually proportional to its floor area, so smaller stations consume less energy
- Smaller numbers of escalators and lifts
- Installing solar panels on the rooves of outdoor stations
- Technology in stations, especially the air conditioning system, that can air condition the station more efficiently

These initiatives can reduce the power consumption in stations by up to 50%, and should be implemented where economically feasible to do so.

Much larger railways may have other facilities to which they need to provide power. Maintenance depots, or large facilities such as washing sheds, can be run from railways power. In some cases workshops, and machine tools such as lathes, can also be run from railways power. This is especially true where the workshop is located in a rail corridor, and away from any other power source or the local power provider.

Providing power to shops on stations is common in Australia, and is a good way to supplement income derived from leasing out parts of the station. It is not possible to find any publicly available information on what railways do in other parts of the world as regards on-selling power, but we can probably make some educated guesses on the conditions that increase the probability that railways on-sell power:
- Railways that consume large amounts of electricity are better equipped to on-sell electricity, those with only diesel trains may not be in a position to do so
- railways would on sell power to shops located on platforms, or wholly within the paid area
- where stations are located in places where there are no other buildings, then the railway is likely to provide the power
- where it is technically challenging to provide power to shops, ie, in a very strange place, the railway may provide the power as the local power company does not have the skills to do it

There are occasionally special situations where a railway may be required to supply power to facilities where there are no other providers. Examples include army facilities, hospitals, hotels and mines located in places where there is no other supply of power. In these cases the railway may need to supply power, and bill for its provision.

It is very difficult to reduce or even manage the power consumed by external parties, towns, workshops, or maintenance facilities. Where the power is supplied, it is not the railway's concern as to the size of the power consumption, unless the power consumed overloads the rail system power grid, in which case the something needs to be done. For reporting purposes any power on-sold should be excluded from any analysis of power consumption. Railways often set targets for energy consumption reduction, and including these makes things very difficult indeed.

Water Consumption in Stations and other Facilities

One of the most important issues with stations is the management of water. Water is needed to maintain basic services, but is also generated from underground stations with seepage through walls. Above ground stations will sometimes need a source of water especially where the station is covered, which will normally come from the local water provider. Stations need to be washed, and large stations have a lot of flat surfaces. Also water is needed for facilities for station staff, and toilets for passengers. Above ground stations may not be covered, so rain will wash any uncovered areas, and only covered areas will need regular washing.

In an underground station, water will seep through walls into the station. Certainly a problem in Australia has been the large volumes of water that are generated from walls of stations and tunnels and can be so large that it begins to become a problem. Whilst having too much water might seem like a good thing, the question arises as to what to do with all this water. Groundwater is full of contaminants, mostly mud or iron oxide (depending on where it is), and this will often need to be removed before the water is put into any river or stormwater drain. Groundwater is often too muddy to be put directly into a river or sea, and will need to be purified before even dumping it into a river. Problems abound with disposing of this water, and it is even possible to clean the groundwater to the point where it is too clean to be added to watercourses, and will kill fish and other wildlife.

Groundwater may be used to provide water for washing and toilets in underground stations. Ordinarily water would not be specifically drained out of the ground to provide for this, as an underground station will have a lot of seepage, which is groundwater, which can be processed into more potable water. Where this is done, some sort of filtration is needed to clean the water, as groundwater is far too dirty in most cases to use even for toilets without some filtration and cleaning. Groundwater looks dirty, which impact upon the appearance of the water but most of the common contaminants are not dangerous.

Alternatively, where a station is above ground, or has a roof, then rainwater may be collected and stored. As with groundwater, rainwater cannot be drunk without processing, but can be used in toilets. Large rainwater tanks can be installed to store this water, which can then be reused. Large stations, with large amounts of roof area, can accumulate very large amounts of water, and this can be used for a variety of different purposes. Water that can be used for washing and toilets, but not drinking is described at non-potable. This dirty water is commonly available, and cause be used quite effectively for a variety of different purposes.

Air Quality in Stations

Underground stations need a constant supply of fresh air to keep the air clean and fresh. People breathe out carbon dioxide and where a station is heavily used then the station will start to smell musty and unpleasant. Part of the management of an underground station is keeping the air fresh.

The best way to keep the station air fresh is to constantly refresh the air with air from the outside. Ventilation can be used to refresh the air, with large fans, often axial fans, pushing the air from the outside in to the station. Even for above ground stations this can sometimes be important, as fully covered stations might need fresh air as well.

Where an underground station is large, the amount of fresh air needed can be very large indeed. Ventilation sizing can be very large, and entire buildings full of ventilation equipment may be needed to put enough air in to keep the station smelling fresh. Power consumed can be substantial, which may reduce the environmental performance of the station overall. There are relatively few alternatives here, but it is possible to ventilate the station naturally, which means the station is open to outside weather. Where outside temperatures and humidity is high, this may not be an attractive option.

It should be noted that station air does not need to be processed before it is pumped into the outside world. Station air is rarely contaminated with anything dangerous, and so does not need to be processed before it is expelled to the outside. This is different to the situation with road tunnels, where road exhaust fumes can accumulate and make any expelled air really filthy, and so the air may need to be scrubbed before it is released into the outside world.

REFERENCES

1. Brons, M & Givoni, M., Rietveld, P. *Access to Railway Stations and its potential in increasing rail use*, Transport Research Part A 43(2009) 136 - 149

2. Transit Cooperative Research Program, *TCRP Report 13 Rail Transit Capacity*, 1996

3. Parsons Brinkerhoff *High Speed Rail*, Network, Issue No 73, Sept 2011, http://www.pbworld.com/news/publications.aspx

4. Chengxiang, Z et al *Research on Train Dwell Time Modelling and Model Application in Metro Station*, 2009 Second International Conference on Intelligent Computation Technology and Automation

5. Kepaptsoglou, K. *A Model for Analyzing Metro Station Platform Conditions Following a Service Disruption*, Annual Conference on Intelligent Transportation Systems, Portugal Sept 2010

6. Battellino, H. *Transport for the transport disadvantaged: A review of service delivery models in New South Wales*, Transport Policy 16 (2009) 123 - 129

7. Schubert, P. *Improving Passenger Security on Urban Rail Networks*, Conference on Rail Engineering, Perth 7-10 September 2008

8. Nicol, J.F. et al. *Comfort Studies of Rail Passengers*, British Journal of Industrial Medicine, 1973, 30, 325 - 334

9. Wiggenraad, P. *Alighting and boarding times of passengers at Dutch railway stations*, Trail Research School, Delft, Dec 2001

10. Lam, W. et al *A Study of Train Dwelling Time at Hong Kong Mass Transit Railway System*, Journal of Advanced Transportation, Vol 32, No 3, pp 285 - 296

11. Chengxiang, Z et al *Research on Train Dwell Time Modelling and Model Application in Metro Station*, 2009 Second International Conference on Intelligent Computation Technology and Automation

12. Transportation Research Board *TCRP Report 13 Rail Transit Capacity*, 1996

13. Harris N G *An international comparison of urban rail boarding and alighting rates*, Proceedings of the Institute of Mechanical Engineers, Vol 221, Part F: Journal of Rail and Rapid Transit 2007

14. Transportation Research Board, *Transit Capacity and Quality of Service Manual Report 100*, 2nd edition, 2003

15. Smith, G. & Ceranic, B. *Spatial Layout Planning in Sub-Surface Rail Station Design for Effective Fire Evacuation*, Architectural Engineering and Design Management, 2008, Volume 4, Pages 99 – 120

16. Williams, R. & Chalmers, G. *Recent Developments in the Design of Cut and Cover Construction for Railway Tunnels and Stations*, Conference on Railway Engineering, Adelaide, May 2000

17. Cheong, SW. *Fire Safety Design for Rapid Transit Systems*, Proceedings of the international conference, Fire India, 2004

18. Lam, W et al *A Study of Passenger Discomfort Measures at the Hong Kong Mass Transit Railway System*, Journal of Advanced Transportation, Vol 33 No3 pp 389 – 399

19. Chen, F. et al *Smoke Control of Fires in Subway Stations*, Theoretical Computer Fluid Dynamics (2003) 16: 349 - 368

20. Kang, K. *Application of a Code Approach for Emergency Evacuation in a Rail Station*, Fire Technology, 43, 331 – 346, 2007

21. London Underground *Station planning standards and guildelines*, 2012 edition, http://www.persona.uk.com/nle/B-Core_docs/G/NLE-G1.pdf

22. Congling, S. et al Modeling and safety of passenger evacuation in a metro station in China, Safety Science(2010) doi:10.1016/j.ssci.2010.07.01

23. Liu, W et al *Modelling Passenger Flow on Stairways in Shanghai Metro Transfer Station*, 2008 International Conference on Intelligent Computation Technology and Automation

Index

Advertising point, 107
Articulation, 13
at grade. *See* Grade separation
Ballast, 60, 61
   Fines, 65
Bangkok Skytrain, 29
bi-level. *See* Double decker
Boardings, 2
Broad gauge, 8
Bus
   Coach, 147
Bus Rapid Transit, 3
Cape gauge, 8
Capping layer, 61
Codeshare, 43
Commuter rail, 35
Concourse, 87
Contact band. *See* wear band
Crossover, 195
Diamond crossover, 195
Diesel multiple units, 41
Double decker, 15
Dwell time, 31, 34, 182
Dynamic gauging, 114
Electric multiple units, 41
Elevators. *See* Lifts
Escalators
   Run-off, 181
Flying junction, 13
Formation, 61
Grade separation, 12
Halts, 5
Headway, 182
Heavy haul, 12
Kinematic envelope, 113
   Centre throw, 120
   End throw, 120
Lifts, 181
Light metro, 28
Load factor, 46

Loading gauge, 113
Metro, 30
   Rubber tyred, 60
Mixed system, 6
Moving walk, 211
Narrow gauge, 8
NFPA 130, 159
Pantograph, 7
Pantograph well, 119
Passenger information systems, 37
Platform length, 77
Portal, 71
Rail
   Tram, 64
Rail cruise, 49
Regional rail, 39
Rollingstock
   Articulation, 120
   Bogie, 120
Route length, 3
Running direction, 192
Russian gauge, 8
Sleeper carriage, 49
Sleepers, 61
St Pancreas station, 221
Stabling, 4
Standard gauge, 8
Station
   Interchange, 77
Stations
   Concourse, 89
   Halt, 82
   Island platform, 80
   Level of service, 175
   Paid area, 87
   Side platform, 79
   Spanish solution, 88
   Vending machine, 80
Stopping pattern, 37

Structure gauge, 113
Supercrush loads, 187
Superelevation, 112, 128
Terminus, 77
Track length, 3
Traction power
  AC, 7
  DC, 7
Trams
  Powerhouse, 6

Tram-train system, 14
Transit centre, 146
Transport Orientated
  Development, 138
Tunnels
  Escape, 164
  Ventilation, 72
Unwired. *See* Traction Power
Wear band, 63
Working timetable, 99

www.ingramcontent.com/pod-product-compliance
Lightning Source LLC
Chambersburg PA
CBHW031413290426
44110CB00011B/364